FRENCH CANADIANS

An Outsider's
Inside Look at Québec

MICHEL
GRATTON

KEY PORTER BOOKS

Canadian Cataloguing in Publication Data

Gratton, Michel
  French Canadians

ISBN 1-55013-438-8 (hc)
ISBN 1-55013-443-4 (pb)

1. Canadians, French-speaking.*   2. Canada — English-French relations.   I. Title.

FC136.G76 1992   971'.004114   C92-094704-2
F1027.G76 1992

The publisher gratefully acknowledges the assistance of the Canada Council and the Ontario Arts Council.

Key Porter Books Limited
70 The Esplanade
Toronto, Ontario
Canada   M5E 1R2

Typesetting: Computer Composition of Canada Inc.

Printed on acid-free paper

Printed and bound in Canada

92 93 94 95 96   6 5 4 3 2 1

CONTENTS

ಠ ಠ ಠ

To my father, Jean-Jacques: It has been a long time since I said I love you

PREFACE

৵ ৵ ৵

Writers of books like this often begin by acknowledging the hundreds of people they interviewed in the course of their research. Such acknowledgments lend immediate authority to the author's purpose; sometimes they even impress critics.

I wish I could say that I spent years interviewing people in order to write this book. Unfortunately, it wouldn't be true. It also wouldn't be me.

That doesn't mean I didn't sweat over what you are about to read. Quite the contrary. I found the task of trying to put down on paper my people, the French Canadians, agonizing. There is nothing more difficult, no duty more demanding, than committing to print the essence of your own people, your own life.

For one thing, it's tempting to focus on the glamour and mystique, the positive side of one's history. But the more I wrote, the more I felt I had to confront the flaws of my people, past and present.

I have no doubt that I will be harshly criticized by some, branded a traitor to "la cause." But I hope that the clear-thinking among you will understand that the views I express here come, first and foremost, from a person who, with all his faults and prejudices, deeply loves his heritage and wants to keep it alive, while weeding out its ugly side.

Others — many, no doubt, and on both sides of the linguistic and cultural border — will find in what follows fodder for their reactionary attitudes. I know this, and I can live with it.

But I couldn't live with myself, as a writer, if I didn't tell this story as I see it. If I can't speak openly about where I come from, what I'm all about, then who am I?

Good question. Technically speaking, I am a Franco-Ontarian, born and raised. I was educated in Québec for a while, and later lived there, but moved back to Ontario. Since then I have worked in the Prime Minister's Office and for two English-language papers. A Franco-Ontarian in Québec, a francophone working in an anglophone milieu — I know what it's like to be an outsider in both of the solitudes.

A word about the focus of this book: it is not intended to be comprehensive, either historically or geographically. It is, rather, one man's portrait of a people. I have concentrated on Franco-Ontarians and Québécois because I know them best, but also because they exemplify the two French Canadas: the first an embattled minority surrounded by English; the other a majority, at least in their own province. Over the years, our struggles have taken different paths — inevitably, given political and geographical realities. But I still see Québécois as French Canadians, my brothers and sisters. And my focus on Québec reflects the fact that, for all French Canadians, Québec is the *sine qua non*. Without it, there isn't much hope for the rest of us.

My heart may be French, and I was once a separatist,

but I have become a Canadian by choice. I think Canada is the way of the future, for my children and for all French Canadians, including Québécois.

Some of you among the English majority have seen us as menacing aliens in your midst. We are anything but. We are from here, just as you are. The politicians call us "distinct." I can live with that adjective. This book is an attempt to capture that distinctiveness, to explain it to English Canadians, without in any way diluting it or turning it into a harmless Walt Disney tourist attraction.

Since our defeat on the Plains of Abraham we have lived in fear — fear of the English, fear of obliteration, and, as I hope to show, fear of ourselves. I long for the day when I can wake up and say, as a Franco-Ontarian songwriter so aptly put it, that we have found "notre place," our place, in this country. I long for the day when my people will no longer be afraid, because we will have allies — English-speaking Canadians — on our side.

I am dreaming, of course. But that is one of my basic faults. This book, then, is the fruit of my vision, and mine alone. And so, no, it didn't take me hundreds of interviews to write it. Just a lifetime.

Mille fois merci to my agent, Helen Heller, who guided me through another lonely adventure. My gratitude and admiration to David Kilgour, whose editing talents will humble any author. *Merci beaucoup* to the Vanier Library and its director-general, Liliane Pinard, for her cooperation and for building a class facility against all odds in a very small town. Thank you very much, my friend John Paton of the *Sun*, for giving me the idea that this book was worth writing: If all Canadians were like you, Canada would not have a problem. Special thanks to Lise Quirouette, whose computer wizardry covered up my clumsiness. Thank you, also, my older sister Ginette, for always taking care of me, and my younger sister, Lucie, for always taking care of me. Thanks again to my favourite partner in crime, John Waterfield, who was there, as before, whenever I needed his help. My apologies and my love to the girls, Valérie, Marie-France, Brigitte, and Shylah, for the lost weekends and my shifting moods. Love and kisses to my friend and wife, Christine, for putting up with a basket case. *Merci* to those francophones who confided in me, and to the authors whose works were crucial to my writing. But most of all, *merci beaucoup* to all those French Canadians who kept the faith and refused to let a culture die, and to all who fight on. Live long and prosper, my friends.

ROOTS AND BATTLE SCARS

?● ?● ?●

UNTIL THAT FATEFUL DAY, in 1959, English was as unknown to me as puberty.

I was seven years old, in grade two, at Baribeau Elementary School, a francophone Catholic school in an area of Ottawa which was then called Eastview. Mrs. Lebrun was my teacher.

About a decade later, this one-square-mile town squeezed between the Rockcliffe Park millionaires' mansions to the north and the Rideau River to the west, and hemmed in by the city of Ottawa to the east and south, would be renamed Vanier, a change that reflected the fact that the majority of its population were francophone.

Eastview was a modest French ghetto, populated by close to 25,000 people at its peak — a glorious day because it was then considered officially a city. But neither I nor my friends, brothers, and sisters knew we were living on a demographic island in a sea of anglophones. We certainly didn't worry about it. We thought it was a great place to live; we didn't think we were different from anybody else living in bigger cities or in the country. In fact, we thought we had it all, and as much of a chance of making it as anybody else.

I did speak a little English, because two doors down from our home, on what was then John Street — later renamed Avenue Deschamps, after my mother's family — lived an Irish family, the Logues. They didn't speak French, or at least if they did, I never heard them do so.

I was impressed by the Logue kids, mainly because they were older and were allowed to play football in the middle of the street — something my parents would never have let me or my brothers do. We didn't associate much with them, and our intelligence reports were limited to the fact that they attended mass at Assumption Church — the English one.

There was also the McCann family, on Carillon Street, one block over. Everybody called the locally famous father by his nickname, "Bunny," and the large family was known for its natural musical talents; they sang and played instruments regularly at French and English community events. But, as far as I was concerned, Bunny's real claim to fame was that, when he and my mother, Cécile, were kids, he had once chased her, wielding a knife. When she reached home, crying and screaming bloody murder, her parents investigated, only to discover that the dangerous weapon was made of plastic. My mother liked to tell the story, even though it made her look silly, because Bunny had become popular in Eastview over the years.

I guess the Logues and the McCanns were, for me, simply objects of curiosity — different, but just as much a part of the French community as the Portuguese family at the end of the street who spoke French. We never stopped to think about the unilingual English street signs or by-laws. After all, every policeman on the local force was French. Only later would I learn about the public and covert fights my forefathers had waged to keep our language alive.

This was my world, my Ontario, until the day Mrs. Lebrun sent me on an errand to the principal's office.

On the way back to my class, I happened to pass the eighth-grade classroom. The door was open, and I could see and hear what was going on inside.

The teacher was walking back and forth at the front of the classroom, speaking in a loud voice, with a book in his hand. He was giving an English spelling test.

To say I was horrified is to put it mildly. For the first time in my short life, I realized that to get through school, I would have to learn this strange and alien language.

For the rest of the day, it was all I could think about, and with every passing minute the prospect grew more terrifying.

That night, when I got home, I burst into tears. My mother figured something terrible must have happened in school; perhaps my nemesis, Philippe Dufour, had been beating up on me again.

I was an A student. Admitting academic defeat was something I could not bear to do, but I summoned the courage to tell my mother I could never graduate from elementary school, because I didn't know English.

She consoled me by explaining that my father and she had learned English too and that I shouldn't worry about it; that, like everything else, it would come in time.

I wasn't convinced. For the first time in my life, I felt different and afraid. Without really knowing it, I had suffered my first culture shock as a member of a minority. I somehow sensed that learning English was not simply an interesting exercise, but a matter of survival. All I knew was school. And I knew I had to do well, to be first in my class, because my parents had frequently reminded me that my mother had skipped two grades and my father three in what we called "la petite école." I was expected to do the same, and eventually I did. I skipped grade three — which explains why my cursive handwriting is as bad as a doctor's — and grade six. Mrs. Lebrun taught me my first course in English during the summer so I could make it to grade four from her class.

By grade eight, I could pass a spelling and grammar test in English, but, as incredible as it may seem to Franco-Ontarian kids today, I couldn't really speak English.

I remember, for instance, the first time I was allowed to go to the Central Canada Exhibition on my own with a friend. I had to know what time it was, since we were scheduled to be picked up at a precise hour and we'd better be there or else . . .

I asked at least five different English-speaking people "What hour is it?" — a literal translation of "Quelle heure est-il?" — before someone finally figured out, when I gestured at my wrist, what I wanted to know. "Oh, you want to know the time," the man said, with a smile. I turned red with embarrassment, realizing I had made a complete fool of myself. I was humiliated and I wonder sometimes today, when I hear so often of Québec suffering "humiliation," if a lot of the feeling doesn't come from such old personal experiences lodged in the subconscious mind.

That feeling, an inferiority complex that followed me through adolescence and beyond, is one I do not like to recall or admit to. But, for a long time, it was there and, I suspect, it's the way many young Franco-Ontarians like myself felt as they confronted the difficulty of maintaining their mother tongue against incredible odds.

At the same time, curiously, we had pride in who and what we were. Eastview was far from being a rich neighbourhood, but few of us saw what statistics would show in later years — that the average salary per household was lower there than almost anywhere else in the Ottawa area. It's even worse today, as the neighbourhood where I still live suffers from an overload of welfare cases drawn by the cheap rents charged by slum landlords with little interest in urban redevelopment. There is still pride, but it is eroding, as most of those of my generation have sought refuge for their families in the safer, cleaner suburbs.

We were a family of seven kids; my older sister was born in January 1952 and I in December of the same year, followed by four brothers and another sister. I was happy when the fifth son was born because my brothers and I now had a complete hockey line.

But I guess the birth I remember most fondly was that of the fourth boy. My mother phoned from the hospital and asked me what name she should give him. At the time I had been fascinated by the election of a new Pope in Rome and marvelled at the pictures, in the French equivalent of *Life* magazine, *Paris-Match*, of the red-robed Cardinals who were in line for the ultimate job on the planet — one of them being our own Cardinal Paul-Emile Léger of Montréal. We were, of course, Catholics. Protestants, followers of the only other so-called religion I knew about at the time, were simply pagans to us. How else could it be when their church steeples didn't even bear a cross? John XXIII's election was announced with the traditional white smoke and, when Maman phoned from the hospital, I wanted my newest brother to be called "Jean XXIII." To my great sadness, I had to settle for Jean-Pierre.

It took me some time to realize that other people considered us to be a huge family. A family of seven children was nothing compared to the Leducs, two streets away, who had seventeen mouths to feed and a house no bigger than ours. My brothers and I slept in one room on two bunks and a small bed, my two sisters in a smaller room.

I have mainly fond memories of childhood, the best being those of playing hockey with my brothers in the makeshift twenty-foot-by-twenty-foot rink behind our house. Summers were a little harder on my parents, because no matter how they tried to sod or grow flowers in the backyard, my brothers and I managed to create devastation. I remember my grandfather Ovila Deschamps, a great gardener himself, looking at our destructive achievements and gasping: "It looks like the Plains of Abraham!" That was the first time I heard about the battle that had transformed our lives as a French-speaking people in North America.

Eventually, my father got fed up and paved the whole thing. That was fine with us. It was easier to make a rink in the winter, and we could boast about having the only paved backyard in Eastview.

We never spoke English in the house. Any attempt to do so was met with a stern warning from our parents — my father especially. I couldn't quite understand what I considered to be an overreaction on his part. Half the time I didn't even know what language I was speaking; I was just trying to imitate something I'd heard other kids say in school.

Our daily paper was *Le Droit*, and I read French comics and magazines from France — *Tintin* and *Pilote*. We didn't watch English television either, save "The Ed Sullivan Show" (except the night Elvis Presley was on), "Bonanza" (because Lorne Greene was a Canadian), and movies (most of which aired late at night after we kids had gone to bed). The big television nights were Mondays and Saturdays. On Monday, the whole family would watch the only game show we knew about — "La poule aux oeufs d'or" ("The Hen That Laid the Golden Egg") — followed by the drama series "Les belles histoires des pays d'en-haut" ("Beautiful Stories from the Northern Country, the Laurentians"), which we called "Seraphin" for short, after the central character, a miser who represented all that was evil in French-Canadian society. On Saturdays, we watched "Hockey Night in Canada," or "La soirée du hockey." But this wasn't true of every French child my age. Many of my classmates would discuss English programs I'd never heard of, and to this day I'm still stumped by "Leave It to Beaver" questions when playing Trivial Pursuit. We knew "Father Knows Best" as "Papa a raison" and "My Friend Flicka" as "Mon ami Flicka."

In school, history taught us quickly that the defeated French were the good guys, and the British the bad. Our heroes were therefore predictable. At the top of the hero hit parade was Adam Dollard des Ormeaux "and his sixteen companions" who had made a heroic stand in a small fort at the Long Sault against nine hundred Iroquois and prevented an all-out attack on Montréal. As the story went, fuelled by nationalist historian l'Abbé Lionel Groulx, Dollard and his handful of men lost only because a lighted powder-keg thrown over the fort wall hit a tree branch and fell inside, killing most of the brave

Frenchmen. The Iroquois were so impressed by the courage of Dollard that they decided not to attack Ville-Marie after all. It would be many years before that myth was debunked and we discovered that our great hero and his bunch were not very welcome in the community anyway, since they were rowdy "coureurs de bois" who wreaked havoc everywhere they settled.

There was also the great "discoverer" of Canada, Jacques Cartier, who in fact was only following the route Basques fishermen had found long before him. Samuel de Champlain was as close as we came to a genuine hero, but our teachers seemed more interested in his military victories over the "evil" Iroquois than in his mapping of New France. Governor Louis de Buade, Compte de Frontenac, was a big star, because he had told a British captain attacking Québec that he would answer his emissaries "with the mouth of my cannons." And of course, there were the "eight Canadian martyrs," Jesuit missionaries tortured and killed by the "cannibalistic" Iroquois, who finally yielded when Frontenac kicked the hell out of them.

As for the Marquis Louis-Joseph de Montcalm, of Plains of Abraham fame, he had just been unlucky. Besides, we had gotten even by killing James Wolfe.

We had our heroines too — Jeanne Mance, Marie d'Youville, and Marguerite Bourgeoys. But the most courageous was Marie-Madeleine de Verchères, the fourteen-year-old girl who had single-handedly scared away a horde of Iroquois — them again! — by lighting several torches in her father's stockade for an entire night to create the illusion that it was heavily defended until help arrived the next day from Ville-Marie. In comparison, Laura Secord was just a chocolate-box trademark.

The only "acceptable" hero of the English regime was

Lieutenant-Colonel Charles-Michel de Salaberry, who, with a regiment of only 1,600 French-Canadian "Voltigeurs" ("light-infantrymen"), had repelled the attack of some 4,200 American troops at Chateauguay, in 1813. De Salaberry was Canadian-born and from the Québec suburb of Sillery. No one mentioned then that he had also fought against Napoléon.

Such teachings, I would understand later, were not simply born of ignorance. They were part of a deliberate plan to resist francophone assimilation and cultural extermination. To a certain extent the plan worked. But that's for a later chapter.

As a child, I counted myself among the lucky ones, mainly because my father owned a variety store and could get everything at cost price. It wasn't quite a general store — we didn't sell clothing or groceries — but more like an up-scale smoke-shop.

My grandfather Salomon Gratton, who rarely admitted to coming from the Québec side of the Ottawa River (Hull and Buckingham), had founded the shop in 1920. It was famous for its school supplies, mainly textbooks that French Catholic elementary schools couldn't get anywhere else. That boondoggle, though, came to an end when the government began supplying separate schools with the necessary texts, and Salomon was stuck with a basement full of school books he couldn't sell or return. In the years to come, my father, an only child who inherited the business, would often cite that business mistake to explain the eventual downfall of the store at 303 Montreal Road. When it went bankrupt in 1967, my father had sixty-three dollars in his pocket and a family of seven to feed. They took away the family car, a red Ford Fairlane station-wagon, the only new car my father had ever owned. I remember the "curé" gave us fifty dollars, and the Emmaus Disciples delivered food after sundown, so the neighbours wouldn't notice. But somehow, the family never lost hope, never felt desperate. Life went on.

Montreal Road was Eastview's main thoroughfare, known to the English as "Gasoline Alley" because of all the gas stations on the one-mile stretch between Cummings Bridge and St. Laurent Boulevard. The only time Eastview die-hard Liberals ever voted Conservative provincially was when the Tory candidate promised to pave Montreal Road — and did. Following that, it was perfectly acceptable for Vanier francophones to vote Liberal federally and Conservative in Queen's Park — although they eventually reverted back to their Liberal roots provincially too.

As my mother's father, Ovila, used to sing: "On vote pour Laurier ou on ne vote pas; on est Canadien ou bien on l'est pas" ("You vote for Laurier or you don't vote; you're a Canadian or you're not"). Laurier was, of course, Sir Wilfrid Laurier, and, for my grandfather, being "Canadien" meant you weren't English, les Anglais, the invaders from across The Pond.

As much as I was proud of my father's status, though — even after the bankruptcy — I was also impressed by my friends Paul and Marc Madore's father. He worked for Canadian Tire, in Hull. I went there once with my buddies from across the street. I'd never seen such a big store with such neat stuff — the bicycles especially — in my life.

Eastview was as insular as it was small. We prided ourselves on our five Catholic parishes — Assumption being the only English one. We had our schools, our nuns to run them, and our priests to make sure everything was done the way God wanted it. God, of course, like Santa Claus, was French, Catholic, male, and white.

The first black man I saw in the flesh appeared in my father's store. I was old enough at the time to feign indifference, but my brother Jean-Pierre, who must have been about five or six, was also there. As he lifted his eyes from the comic book he couldn't read, he looked as if he'd just seen an apparition. I could feel my father cringe as Jean-Pierre went around the counter and started circling the customer like a cat, staring intently at his face. Finally, Jean-Pierre exclaimed, "Hey, Dad! That's a Negro!" In fact, the French word he used was "nègre," which is a little closer to "nigger."

How could he know any better when one of the only English rhymes we knew was: "Eeny, meeny, miny, mo, catch a nigger by the toe . . ." The only pictures of black people we'd seen had been brought back by missionaries like my uncle Gérard, who was sent to Papua New Guinea by the Montfortains Order to evangelize what we were told were cannibals. He was following in the footsteps of the Jesuit martyrs Pope Pius XI had canonized in 1930.

Like blacks, sex and its perversions simply did not exist in our world. God brought children into the world, just as the Virgin Mary had become pregnant through the Holy Ghost. In school, for instance, like all good Catholic children, we learned our "Petit catéchisme" ("Little Catechism"), which listed everything you apparently needed to know about religion, starting with the difference between a mortal and a venial sin. There were also the "Seven Capital Sins." I never quite figured out whether they were venial or mortal. The teachers made it sound as if they could be both. And, of course, we had to learn the Ten Commandments, though in fact we were taught only nine of them. Throughout elementary school, successive teachers skipped the seventh one, because it had to do with something they said we would "learn later." That commandment, of course, concerned sex out of wedlock.

I remember one progressive teacher in grade eight going beyond the school curriculum to try to explain to his all-male class what might be happening to their growing bodies. (The girls were separated from the boys both in the classroom and in the school yard, so I have little idea what happened on their side of the sexual divide.) His lecture was so vague I had trouble understanding it.

It was only in high school, about a year later, that my friend Jean-Pierre, at my request, told me the facts of life in a conversation I insisted should be absolutely private. When he explained how babies were made, my initial reaction was to protest that my parents would never do anything like that. True, I was more innocent than most, but where did I come by my innocence? I don't blame my parents: they were more tolerant than most. I remember, for instance, my mother telling me later in life how she had to give an older girl on the street sanitary napkins because her parents refused to accept or explain why she had started to menstruate, and her mother insisted that she simply put rags in her underwear to soak up the blood.

The church was the first culprit in this narrow-minded righteousness, relying on fear of divine retribution to impose its views of morality on an obedient flock. To a great extent, the ploy worked. The reasoning was easy: without the church and its elite of followers, you didn't have a chance in hell of going very far in life — or so you believed.

We went to church every Sunday and, until the rules were liberalized, didn't eat for three hours or drink for one hour before taking Communion. We were told terrible stories of what happened to those who dared challenge the power of God.

My favourite was the one about the evil man who had deliberately kept his host in his mouth after Communion. After mass, he intended to prove the host wasn't the body of Jesus Christ. So, before a crowd of parishioners, he spit it out on the church steps and stepped on it. Then he watched in terror as blood seeped from what was to him just a thin piece of bread.

Heavy stuff for a child. Nobody seemed to stop and think that the host would have melted in his mouth long before the mass was over.

Then there's the famous French-Canadian legend of the farmer from Rigaud, not too far from the Ontario border, along Highway 40 to Montréal. He decided to plough his field on a Sunday, despite warnings from the cure that he would suffer the wrath of divine providence for his actions. His potato field, as the story of the miracle went, was turned to stone. The plateaux of Rigaud are still there, and the stones do look like so many potatoes. But they were left there by glaciers during the last Ice Age.

The scariest story, though, had to be the punishment connected with compulsory Communion at Easter. According to legend, if you went for seven consecutive years without taking Communion on the commemorative day of Christ's resurrection, you would be changed into a "loup-garou," a sort of French-Canadian werewolf.

But the religious leaders had more than one trick in their bag to embarrass us into submission. One of them was "la dîme" ("the tithe"), the minimum amount every family was expected to pay the parish annually, on top of the regular Sunday "quête," or "collection," when the top parishioners, known as "marguilliers" ("churchwardens"), would fan out in the aisles, sometimes up to three times, to rake in the money.

Once a year, the *curé* would get up into his pulpit and list the names of those who had not paid their *dîme*, which was to be the equivalent of one day's salary. All the names and amounts given were also posted at the entrance to the church. My father remembers his father checking it out and commenting on the amount given by a big local contractor: "He must have had a bad year; he gave only twenty dollars."

I can't dissociate my childhood from priests and religion. Both were everywhere. Like many in my school, I was an altar boy. It wasn't so bad on Sundays, when the senior altar boys would serve mass, and we'd just sit on our assigned benches, wearing soutanes that made us look like so many miniature priests. It was a little trickier, though, during the week, when you had to serve the daily morning mass at 7:00 and consequently learn every reply to the priest's prayer — in Latin. The Confiteor was the tough part. It was an interminable prayer, and the altar boy was expected to recite it all in the defunct language while on his knees with his head bowed. I struggled through the first few times until I figured out what the older, more experienced boys were doing. They'd just wing it, say a few words at the beginning and the end, and mumble the rest. I was surprised to find out it worked brilliantly, although I doubt it ever fooled any of the priests. And we were paid one quarter a mass to do this — which was still a lot less than the old man who sang the hymns or the woman who played the organ got.

Because my uncle was a bishop, the youngest ever to be ordained in Canada at the time, I was expected to follow in his footsteps. And that meant, during the summer months, serving daily mass at the nuns' convent at 6:30 a.m. The nuns were nicer but cheaper — only a dime a mass. I have to admit there were mercantile reasons behind my volunteering for the job: it got me my first bicycle, since there was no way I could make it on foot to the convent fast enough.

The biggest religious event of the year was the "Procession de la Fête-Dieu," something comparable to the Orange Parade for Protestants. If you'd been a good altar boy that year, you got to wear a red soutane and carry a large candlestick, flanking the priest and the Holy Sacrament through the streets of the city, papal flags flying everywhere. If we were really lucky the "Pontifical Zouaves," the local marching band, in their Vatican Army uniforms, would also be part of the parade. My grandfather Deschamps's proudest moment came the year his house was chosen to be the "reposoir," a pit stop or resting-place where the church would set up a special temporary altar. He hung his several rosaries from the altar that day. After all, it was a glorious moment for a man who attended church every morning and recited his rosary faithfully every night with Montréal's Cardinal Léger on CKCH Radio, a francophone station broadcasting from Hull but picking up the Cardinal's signal from Montréal.

Priests were everywhere in our lives. The Montfortains from Notre-Dame-de-Lourdes — my uncle's order — were regular visitors for dinner on Saturday nights.

They and my parents would play card games, mostly Five Hundred, all evening.

The vicar of Notre-Dame-du-St-Esprit came home to teach piano to my older sister, Ginette, who, thanks to him, once won first prize at the Ottawa Conservatory annual competition. The French daily paper *Le Droit* hadn't bothered to cover the event, thinking that since there was only one French-Canadian entry in the group she had no chance of winning. When she did, a reporter and a photographer came to our place, and Ginette was famous for a day. We all shared in the glory.

The vicar also organized the weekly bingo game and eventually had a hockey rink built behind Baribeau Elementary School. He formed the first hockey league for kids, but in those days, there didn't seem to be much difference between players of pee-wee, bantam, and midget age.

Being among the youngest, I was totally outclassed, but I loved the game so much it didn't matter. I would dress up in full uniform — in a Canadiens sweater, of course — and walk about half a mile to the rink . . . with my skates on. I couldn't tighten the laces myself. Maman had to do it. By the time I got to the rink, though, I was already exhausted, my blades dull from the sand and the salt on the sidewalk, and the laces too loose to support my ankles. In my first official league hockey game, I was knocked out by a puck. My Canadiens tuque offered little protection.

I had a lousy season. At the end of it, at a party in the church basement, the *curé* asked me how many goals I had scored. I said I hadn't any, but I'd gotten one assist. I lied. I had to confess about it later, but I made sure I did so to the vicar rather than the *curé*.

Such was life in Eastview, and we rarely ventured out of it.

We did have some regular family outings — on Saturday nights, for example. After all the kids had taken their baths and donned their pyjamas, before the 8:00 p.m. hockey game, we'd all get in the car and drive around Rockcliffe Park to look at the mansions we could never afford. My mother would often point out Dr. Denis Desjardins's house. He was a local boy who had made it big. Maybe, some day, her kids would too.

On Sundays, we'd go on picnics in Rockcliffe or Vincent Massey Park, often with my uncle and aunt Gilles and Gisèle Lalonde. Gisèle was later to become one of the most famous mayors of Vanier. Some summers, we rented a cottage, but never too far from town, because my father had to take care of the store, which closed at 10:00 p.m. We went to Constance Bay, Witchwood, or Clarence Creek, now all built-up suburbs of the capital.

I vaguely remember train trips to Montréal, where we would shop at Lalonger for my sisters' clothes and Dupuis Frères for anything else. One of my most terrifying moments came in the latter store, when I found myself suddenly separated from my parents. I ran through the aisles, screaming hysterically, until an old woman grabbed me by the arm. She spoke English. Where was Bill 101 when I needed it? I struggled out of her grasp and ran like hell until I eventually found my mother.

Other than that, Eastview remained the centre of the universe. We knew that Lower Town, just the other side of the Rideau, was a French area, but we were taught not to associate with kids from that "bad" neighbourhood. In fact, most of East Lower Town was a poor district, with clapboard houses that were eventually levelled by the city. But the western part of it was of a much higher class than our own neighbourhood. We knew of Sandy Hill, "La Côte-de-Sable," but that was the domain of French doctors and lawyers. We never suspected that, beyond Parliament Hill, in Ottawa West, Mechanicsville was also a French ghetto, although every Christmas we would travel to St-François d'Assise church to see the most famous and biggest crèche in the region.

My parents in their youth had rarely travelled beyond the two miles that separated us from Parliament Hill. We were the same. Ottawa West was English and alien. We simply didn't go there, as if some force field existed that told us we weren't welcome. It was only in my twenties that I realized how built up that section of the city was. Even in my older childhood years, my reflex was to avoid it like the plague.

As for the Québec side, Hull, like Lower Town, was a place for children from not-so-good families who all worked for the E.B. Eddy match company. Gatineau was the home of girls who chewed gum, smoked on the street, and swore. Thurso smelled, thanks to its stinking pulp mill, and would not redeem itself until the 1970s when a hockey superstar by the name of Guy Lafleur emerged from the village.

Papineauville, a little farther down Highway 148, on the Québec side of the Ottawa River, was, however, a fine place. That was because it housed the seminary where my uncle the bishop had been a student. And that was where I was slated to go after graduation from grade eight, along with my friend Bernard — whose father had attended the same boarding-school — and Robert, another friend from our parish.

At eleven years of age, a member of an embattled but

solid francophone minority, I was not quite ready for the Québec culture shock that was to hit me there.

The three years I was to spend in boarding-school were, in retrospect, pivotal in the evolution of my view of Canada; of the place of francophones in that political entity; and, mostly, of Québec and the Québécois.

I want to describe them because the seminary I went to — and its teachings — were not that different from all the "collèges classiques" many Québécois attended in those years before and at the outset of the Quiet Revolution that eventually made many of those institutions obsolete. Those people were to become the Québec elite of the last four decades of the century, the baby-boomers who would make or break Confederation, if only because they had the numbers.

First, let me explain that most of the boys of my generation who attended the seminary in Papineauville, about forty miles from Ottawa, on the Québec shore of the river, had little or no intention of ever becoming priests. The religious calling that had once made so many French-Canadian families proud of their sons and daughters was a thing of the past. Without knowing it, our generation was already headed in a direction that would make us more than just the cheap labour force Lord Durham had deplored more than a century earlier. A lot of us faked the desire to find "la vocation," but most had made the decision early on that celibacy was not our idea of a party, and certainly not an ideal in life.

For many — those from Ottawa river towns like Thurso, Plaisance, Ripon, and Montebello, for instance — the Papineauville seminary was simply the closest good school to attend. For those who came from farther away, in places where the Montfortains priests did their recruiting, it was cheaper than many other colleges, and it was a chance for sons of farmers or lumberjacks to attain a higher education than they could otherwise aspire to.

For me, well, there was, of course, my uncle Gérard's success story and the fact that the Montfortains from Notre-Dame-de-Lourdes parish were regular visitors at home. But if it hadn't been Papineauville, I would still have ended up in some private institution, because there was no way I could retain real fluency in French in any Ontario public high school at the time.

In those days I didn't know how important that last part of the equation was. It was simply a given in my family that places like Eastview and Rideau High were not quite right. The prevailing opinion was that only "bums" went there.

In fact, it was the English influence my parents really feared most from the Ontario public-school system they knew only too well. My parents had kept their language and culture by attending private schools too, despite the fact that their parents could barely afford the luxury. The public system was a one-way ticket to assimilation. Sending one's children to private school was not a universal practice, but certainly widespread among the French, who were taught by their church leaders that "qui perd sa langue, perd sa foi" ("he who loses his language, loses his faith"). Since losing your Catholic beliefs at the time meant risking excommunication, it was not something my parents and others like them would contemplate. Not all Franco-Ontarian families reacted like mine did. In fact, most didn't, which contributed largely to the gradual assimilation of the province's francophones before things started to change at the public-school level.

My parents certainly never suspected how badly I would be received in the Québec institution; otherwise they might have opted instead for an Ontario private school like the de La Salle Académie in Ottawa's Lower Town that my father attended. To this day, I've never raised the matter with them.

Boarding-school was not a place where you complained. You simply learned to survive and not disappoint those who worked hard to pay to send you there.

Being from Ontario, I was immediately branded an outsider by my fellow students. We were the equivalent of the "maudits Anglais," the "têtes carrées" ("squareheads"). I learned for the first time the expression "vendus," which literally means "sold" and refers to those francophones who have "sold out" to the English majority. For many of my fellow students, every francophone from Ontario was exactly that, "un vendu."

They used to mock my home town by calling it "Eastview, la cité des égoûts," which literally means "sewer city." The term referred to the fact that our sewer system had a nasty habit of overflowing in the spring, on Montreal Road, right in front of the Montfortains' church. But it was another easy put-down that, at first, made me feel I didn't belong.

In the three years I spent in the school, I don't think I ever quite understood the Québécois reaction to my provincial origins. Until that day, I had not known that being French in one province was different from being French in another. And I certainly was not aware of the social and political forces that were already at work in

Québec and would send shock waves through the whole country in the years to come.

I knew vaguely of a former premier named Maurice Duplessis, but my opinion of the man was limited to the few words I'd heard my father or mother speak about him: first, he was a bad and backward man who ruled Québec like a quasi dictator; second, he had made a lot of trouble for a bishop called Monseigneur Charbonneau, who had given his sacred ring to my uncle Gérard when he himself attained that important church status. A bishop's ring was an important symbol in those days. You were expected to kiss it every time you met such a powerful man of the cloth. Most would extend their hand to make sure you would do so, although my uncle, raised in a modest household and still an Eastview boy at heart, was not big on it.

The premier of Québec at that time was Jean Lesage, who was well regarded by my family because he was a Liberal and had been a top minister under Prime Minister Louis St-Laurent. Lesage and his "équipe du tonnerre" (a political slogan meaning he had assembled a team as strong as thunder), was to bring Québec into the modern era after the "Grande Noirceur" ("dark age") of the Duplessis regime. He would be the last Québec premier, Liberal or otherwise, to have solid links with and sympathies towards Ottawa.

This was how things stood in 1964. The Liberals had ended sixteen years of uninterrupted Union Nationale rule four years earlier, and the reforms they had promised were well under way, many piloted by a charismatic former journalist named René Lévesque. He was also liked by my parents because of his weekly Radio-Canada television public-affairs show, "Point de mire" ("Focus"). This incredibly popular one-man show, where

Lévesque would use a blackboard to explain complicated international situations in layman's terms, was largely responsible for making René one of Quebec's great political icons. It is doubtful he ever would have won his first election as a Liberal without it. In my parents' view, the man who would later lead Québec to the verge of separation could do no wrong back then.

For us, though, the most dramatic of the reforms would happen in the educational system, which had long been in need of a major overhaul. A Québec deputy minister by the name of Arthur Tremblay would be largely responsible for it and can be considered one of the fathers of the Quiet Revolution that radically transformed Québec and its people. Tremblay, a simple man blessed with a superior intellect, would later be appointed to Canada's Senate during Joe Clark's short-lived tenure as prime minister in 1979. He was considered to be one of the country's top constitutional experts and, although very "nationaliste," in the Québécois sense of the word — meaning he strongly believes the people of Quebec are a nation in their own right — he was also a federalist. He became a good friend of mine during his years in Ottawa and an invaluable source of information on the history and evolution of Québec.

But in those days, with the priests who saw their stranglehold on education loosening dangerously, he was not a very popular man. When Daniel Johnson campaigned against Lesage in 1966, one of his main themes was that he would get rid of the wicked Tremblay once the Union Nationale regained power. The priests who ran the Papineauville seminary were very much on Johnson's side, since the very existence of the institution was threatened from the first day I got there.

Most of the older students who knew something about

politics were also pro-Union Nationale for similar reasons. The massive changes that were taking place in the province did not please every Québécois. Most of the malcontents were from rural Québec, where the Liberals were perceived as representing the big city (i.e., Montréal) and a godless party. As the *curés* used to say in their Sunday sermons during the Duplessis era: "Heaven is blue; Hell is red." Blue was, of course, the colour of the Union Nationale, a child of the defunct provincial Tory party, while the Grits' colour was bright red.

I remember vividly that when Lesage was narrowly defeated — fifty-five to fifty-one seats — in 1966, the head priest, known officially as the "discipline prefect," announced it proudly from his pulpit at breakfast in the seminary's refectory. This was the only way we could find out about world events since we were not allowed to watch popular television shows or listen to the radio. Most of the students cheered wildly at the news. I couldn't understand why, since I had been raised to believe the Liberals were the party of the francophones. In Eastview, they gave you a Liberal membership card before your birth certificate. I sat in silence, mesmerized by the reaction of these unpredictable Québécois. What was so important about Daniel Johnson anyway?

Canada would find out soon enough as, a year later, he squared off against a federal justice minister named Pierre Elliott Trudeau and put forward his idea of "equality or independence" — the first real separatist threat ever voiced by the government of Québec in the twentieth century.

His election, though, despite the priests' elation, did not result in the firing of Arthur Tremblay; did not stop the education reforms; and, eventually, turned the seminary into a regional high school for boys *and* girls, a so-called *polyvalente*.

Arthur Tremblay, now seventy-five, still has a vivid memory of those hairy days and how, despite all odds, he survived not only the Johnson regime, but those of Robert Bourassa and René Lévesque.

Tremblay's story of his rise to prominence in the history of French Canada is as close to a fairy tale as you can come. (In passing, there is a running gag about the Tremblays, who are so numerous in Québec they seem to be everywhere, from hockey teams to the boardrooms of industry. *Croc*, the province's incredibly successful humour magazine, once defined the Tremblays as a "horde of Mongols that regularly invade Québec.")

Arthur was the first of fourteen children. His father, Edouard, the oldest in a family of six, started working as a lumberjack at the age of nine. When he was fourteen, Edouard's father died in a freak accident while fishing the St. Lawrence River; so, barely a teenager, Edouard became responsible for the well-being of the family. He took up a lumberjack's job full-time, which meant spending his first winter in the forest of the "Grandes Bergeronnes" with a hardened bunch of "bûcherons" ("lumberjacks").

Edouard couldn't read or write. He could only sign his name. "If he had ever learned, he lost it at age nine in the mountains of the Grandes Bergeronnes. But, as soon as I learned how to read, I would read him the paper," says Arthur Tremblay. He remembers an election in 1930. "There were two candidates in Chicoutimi riding, a Liberal and a Conservative. The Liberal candidate was a real dud. The Conservative was better. Even though I was only thirteen or fourteen, I realized this and I asked my father if he was going to vote Liberal. He said pensively, 'This year it won't be easy.' I praised the other candidate, and he agreed that I was probably right. But it bothered him. He had been a Liberal since Laurier. Election day comes, and he goes to vote, after ending his shift at 4:00 p.m. He comes home for supper, and I ask him, 'You voted for the Conservative?' He said, painfully, 'Well, I was going to vote for him, but I couldn't bring myself to do it.' So I said, 'But, Papa, we both agreed he was the best!' And he replied, 'Yes, but you know, you can't trust those Tories.' Partisanship went deep in those days." Little did Edouard Tremblay know that fifty years later, the son who was reading him the paper would turn up in Ottawa as a Conservative senator. "I had no personal Liberal heritage. My generation, I think, didn't have that sort of blind devotion to a given party. And except for a few 'vieux rouges' or 'vieux bleus' who still remain that way, I believe that partisanship ended with my generation. In any case, it was thanks to my father that I started to turn into a Conservative," he says and laughs.

"I was lucky to be the eldest [since my parents could afford to pay for the seminary]. In families of thirteen or fourteen children like mine, the luckiest were the oldest, the ones in the middle suffered more, and the youngest were again lucky because the oldest ones could pay the cost."

Of all the things Arthur Tremblay told me, this last really struck a chord, because, being the oldest of five boys, I also knew I'd had a better break than those who came after me, and I have always felt guilty about it.

In a "collège classique," in Tremblay's day as in mine, boys attended from grade eight until they had earned the equivalent of a bachelor's degree. The grades didn't have numbers, though; they were known by names related to what you were expected to learn in a given year. Grade eight was "Elément latin," nine "Syntaxe," ten "Méthode," eleven "Versification," twelve "Belles-lettres," thirteen "Rhétorique," fourteen "Philosophie I," and fifteen "Philosophie II." In the last two years, you were deemed so close to being a priest, you were required to wear a soutane.

"I know [my becoming a priest] was the secret hope of my mother," says Arthur. "I was afraid of having, as they called it, 'la vocation.' When my director of conscience [each student in every seminary had one] finally told me he didn't think I had the calling, boy was I happy. I guess they just realized I had no real desire for it, because at the outset, in those days, everyone was expected to have 'la vocation.' "

Despite the Depression, Arthur managed to get into social science at Laval in 1939. Social science led him to become a member of the then-called "Bloc Universitaire" with people like Daniel Johnson and Jean-Jacques Bertrand, who would both later become Union Nationale premiers of Québec. It was a nationalistic movement and greatly innovative for the times.

In 1943, with the help of a philosopher-priest, Tremblay opened the "Ecole de pédagogie" and eventually became the first "career" professor at Laval. His pioneering efforts earned him a scholarship to Harvard, where he got a master's degree in education. He was fuelled by one desire — to keep young people in schools. His research had revealed the astonishing statistic that only 4.5 per cent of the Québec student population, whether they attended a "collège classique" or a public school, made it to university.

There were some major differences between the two systems, the main being that most of the *collèges clas-*

siques were run by priests and had compulsory courses in both Latin and Greek. They were also stronger in the teaching of French, but dismal in mathematics and science subjects — a weakness that would affect me personally in the years to come. The fact was, though, that a student who successfully completed his course at a *collège classique* then had access to all the faculties at a university, whereas graduates from the public-school system could get into only science, engineering, or commerce.

After the war, American intellectuals began to take an interest in Québec and its people. "We had become a subject of interest for the anthropologists," Tremblay chuckles. He happened to meet American education experts who were very interested in the ideas he was proposing for the future of French-Canadian education. So much so, in fact, that in the mid-1950s, Arthur Tremblay, son of a lumberjack who couldn't read or write and a mother who quit school in grade four, got a $115,000 grant from the Carnegie Foundation to pursue his research. Consider that in today's dollars, and the amount is staggering.

After that he entered the political world, something he never really wanted to do, but he realized that it was probably the only way to turn his ideas into reality. He agreed to become special adviser to Jean Lesage's minister of Youth and Public Instruction (a ministry later renamed Education). He would eventually become deputy minister, and it was in that position that he wreaked havoc upon the system.

Under Tremblay's leadership, the two separate systems were combined to create the *polyvalentes* that we have today, combining elements of both the private and the public and offering a greater number of options to the students.

At Papineauville seminary, the younger students like myself knew very little about the amplitude of the revolution that was sweeping the province. In my three years there, the system was strict and religious: every morning began with a wake-up bell at 6:00, followed by prayer and then mass. Then came a half-hour study period before breakfast, because the priests believed most people studied better on an empty stomach — a notion I never quite understood. Classes ran until late afternoon, when we were given a snack before the recitation of the rosary.

At night, after a forty-five-minute recreation period, usually spent playing hockey, football, or baseball, there was another prayer time, followed by one hour of study and finally bedtime.

For some strange reason, weekends as I had known them in Ontario didn't exist in Papineauville. In fact, Sunday was the only real day off, when you were allowed visitors. During the week we got Tuesday and Thursday afternoons off for compulsory sport activities. If our team wasn't scheduled to play, we usually ended up having to referee a game.

For the first two years, nobody was allowed to leave the college, except at Hallowe'en (in Québec, a religious day known as "La Toussaint") for a couple of days, Christmas for ten days, and Easter for five days. The two months of summer vacation were a huge relief.

My parents had warned me I would have to learn discipline and toughness, but I hadn't realized that the seminary would be so regimented. For all the good it may have done for me, I would not wish it on my children. I learned a lot there, but the greatest lesson was probably disobedience.

Students seem to emerge from seminaries either subjugated to authority or rebellious. I'm happy to say I became the latter. And though I was younger than most of my fellow students — and smaller — by my second year I had become one of the leaders of the pack. We regularly devised plans to escape the confines of the school — sometimes in the middle of the night, putting pillows under our sheets — to go to "the village" and hopefully meet girls. Sometimes the older locals would rat on us, and I can remember vividly the times we had to outrun the priests through the fields and the woods to beat the bell for the evening prayer. Getting caught carried the threat of automatic expulsion.

One of our few releases was rock and roll. Because I was from Ontario, my English, though far from perfect, was much better than that of my friends, who could barely say "yes" and "no" in the language. I happened to have a good singing voice and I knew the words to all the songs the others could only guess at. Some of us formed a band. Our first drummer had only empty cardboard boxes to play on, but it didn't matter: we were challenging the authorities, letting our hair grow, wearing bell-bottom pants and polka-dot shirts. It was our own quiet revolution, and it actually had an effect on the seminary. On Saturday nights in my third year, we were permitted to watch "The Monkees" on television and later to listen to current rock-and-roll hits.

The priests tried to sell us on classical music. Today I regret not having paid more attention, but for me rejecting it was another form of protest, especially since the music teacher at some point taught us a song with the refrain "Québec, mon beau pays et mes amours!"

Québec was neither my country nor the love of my life, and I couldn't accept being forced to sing a song praising it, when not being from Quebec had caused me so much aggravation at boarding school. Every time we had to perform it, I'd change "Québec" to "Ontario." Sounds silly today, but back then it seemed important not to have an identity imposed on me.

The fact is, though, that during those crucial three years, which often make the difference in the beliefs you will defend into adulthood, my friends were Québécois. I discovered a whole new society where English barely existed, where the French acted like what they considered themselves to be: the majority. I learned that there were still a lot of people living out on farms like those my grandfathers had left to come to the city. Subconsciously, "they" became my people, the ones I would associate with my culture later in life.

But I had another issue to face. I will always remember the phone call on a Sunday night — one of the few times we were permitted to talk to our parents outside visiting hours. My father asked me if I really wanted to go back to the seminary the next year. And, he added, "We honestly won't mind if you don't."

I thought for a few seconds. I had heard of the changes coming to the school: next year, because of orders from the authorities in Québec City, we would have not only "externs" as fellow students, but girls too! The priests had had to give up their fight for the seminary for two main reasons. First, with the Quiet Revolution a growing number of them were quitting the priesthood, a phenomenon that not so long before would have been a disgrace to every family with a "defrocked" among them.

Second, because of the dwindling numbers of priests, private schools had to hire more lay teachers, and their influence was beginning to change things.

I was afraid of going back to a world I had known only during holidays for the previous three years. It seemed so much had gone on out there that I didn't know about. Would I be a nerd there, whereas here, in Papineauville, I was a kind of king? And then there was simply the disappointment I might cause my family. This was probably my biggest concern and the silliest, since my parents were by this time scrounging every penny to pay my tuition and they must have known that, in my heart, I wanted out.

Tears came to my eyes when I admitted to my father I would rather stay home the following year, and he said, "That's fine." I was the happiest boarder in the seminary for the rest of the year, and several of my friends were envious, since they weren't being given the same choice.

Ontario was as much a shock to me as Québec had been three years earlier. I went to meet with the principal of the Ottawa University High School — another priest. I thought I would be going into grade twelve, since when I had left Eastview's elementary school I had completed grade eight and then spent three years in the seminary. But the principal didn't quite see it that way. According to the Québec system, I was going into the equivalent of grade eleven.

I couldn't believe my ears and I cried foul. Finally the school authorities relented and let me enter grade twelve on the condition that I take two courses, in mathematics and in English, during the summer.

So, there I was, a student used to finishing in the top

three, attending summer school with the kids who had failed courses.

English was bad enough. My years in a Québec school had stalled me at the grade-eight level. I got good marks all right; I could write any test with my eyes closed. But I had learned nothing. I remember reading *Red Badge of Courage* during that summer course and not understanding a word of it. Luckily, since my father still owned a variety store, I had access to "Classics" comic books. With the images and the simple dialogue I could roughly make out what it was all about.

Math was the real shocker. Not only was Ontario far ahead of the *collège classique* model, but algebra — which I'd only heard about — was being taught in English only. There were no French textbooks.

To this day I still believe the mark of 65 I got for that summer course was a measure of the generosity of the teacher, who happened to be a francophone and tried to understand my dilemma.

No matter how hard school was, the hardest part of all was my new social status. Although most of the students at the school were francophones, the "in" thing was to revert to English once you got out to the school yard. I was trying desperately to make new friends, but my awkwardness and extremely noticeable accent in spoken English made me the subject of laughter more than anything else.

In Québec I'd been treated like a "maudit Anglais"; here I was now a "frog."

Yet, instead of speaking French, which I knew everybody understood, I realized instinctively that survival and success now depended on the language of the other majority, the one I'd forgotten about in Québec.

I was humiliated and angry. I wonder how many francophones lived through similar experiences. As for me, I now know that what I went through was a small part of greater events, all of them leading to the day when a settling of scores with the English majority was bound to come. What I didn't know was that someone had tried to settle the score long before most of us were aware of it.

LA PATENTE

ૐ   ૐ   ૐ

WHEN YOU DRIVE OVER St. Patrick's Bridge into Vanier from Ottawa you hit a street called Beechwood.

Although upgraded in recent years, thanks to the yup-
pies who invaded the adjoining communities of New
Edinburgh and Linden Lea — presumably to rub shoul-
ders with the Rockcliffe Park elite — it is a rather innocuous stretch of narrow, winding road.

For a long time its main and only attractions seemed
to be "The Towne" cinema, which catered to the university and rare-film club; the "Joanisse IGA"; and the
"Claude Hotel," a tavern that had outgrown its glory
days long before it was finally levelled in 1990. "The
Towne" has burnt down, and many of the old two- and
three-unit apartment buildings that lined the street have
been gradually replaced by trendy restaurants and bou-
tiques — a transformation I never thought I'd see.

Beechwood, you see, was for years the heart of an
industrial district that centred on a factory called "The
Dominion Bridge," which took up most of the space behind my elementary school and the Rideau River. A rail-
way line used to run through Vanier and the Dominion

Bridge, and right through what was to become the up-scale neighbourhood of New Edinburgh, on the north side of Beechwood Street. The people living in the small, bunched-up houses — many of them duplexes or tri-plexes — surrounding the area were working class.

I mention Beechwood Street because a couple of thou-sand feet from the bridge, near the "S" curve of Hem-lock Road that will take you back to Ottawa on the other side of encircled Vanier, you will come across, on the right side, the Vanier side, of the street, a big, red-brick church whose jurisdiction has always been divided down the middle between Ottawa and my one-square-mile home town.

The church is not very impressive. You will have seen more imposing religious shrines elsewhere in small Québec villages. But its significance for French Cana-dians goes way beyond its dark appearance or the or-dinary street it is located on.

This is St-Charles church, my mother's childhood parish, a fact that is important only because it was the first parish in what was then called Eastview. There, for several decades, a priest named F.X. Barrette reigned supreme. And in his presbytery, on October 22, 1926, along with seventeen other French Canadians, the man known as "le curé Barrette" would form a secret order of resistance fighters who would go on to influence greatly the politics of the city and the whole country.

It was called the Order of Jacques Cartier and would even get an official federal charter in 1927 under the official name "Les Commandeurs de l'Ordre de Jacques Cartier" to protect what were really covert activities. But, to its members, it was known only as "La Patente."

In English, the word means "The Thing" or, if you stretch it a bit, "The Gimmick." The origin of the nickname is lost in the memories of those who closely guarded its secret existence in those days, when, had it become known, it would have been crushed by the then solidly anti-French and anti-Catholic authorities. But, as one former member put it to me, the name came simply from the fact that, when asked by their wives where they were spending their evening, men would answer evasively that they were going to their "Patente." For some other reason, the members were also known as "Pieds Noirs," or "Black Feet" — the only logical explanation for that name being the fact that the Order was largely ruled by the church and that priests customarily wore heavy-soled black shoes.

Over a period of four decades, with its heyday between the end of the Second World War and 1960, La Patente's tentacles reached so far that it could claim to have between 40,000 and 70,000 members. That is quite a few people when you consider that only males could be members and that we are talking about a secret organization.

The Order's initial strength and rapid growth can be attributed to the fact that the structure that enabled it to blossom was already in place when the *curé* Barrette started it — the Catholic church. It had a headquarters, "La Chancellerie," in Ottawa — which in fact was eventually run by the archdiocese — and it spread from one parish to the next. Since the French Catholic church had learned to fend for itself (with help from the Vatican) after the Plains of Abraham, the network was well-established when the time came to make this kind of nearly seditious move.

The men who founded "La Patente" had two main enemies in their sights: first, the Orange Order, the Protestants, whom they considered to be well organized and more than powerful enough to squelch Catholics and by extension the French-Canadian race; and, second, the Irish, whom they suspected of being the "enemy within" since they threatened to take over the church on North American soil and make it an English demesne.

Whatever their deeper motivations were, most of the founders were convinced they had to do something drastic to stop what appeared to be a series of dangerous setbacks as French was banned from schools in Saskatchewan and Manitoba and, in 1913, in Ontario — where Bill 17 created a reaction so strong in the French-Canadian community that it led to the foundation of the daily newspaper *Le Droit* that was to launch my career sixty years later. There were other, less public signs of repression: French Canadians had little chance of being promoted within the federal public service and were victims of widespread discrimination; in stores like Ogilvie's on Rideau Street, for instance, francophones were ordered not to speak their language at work.

But how and why is it that an organization that was to have such an impact on the future of all of French Canada, especially Québec, should begin in, of all places, such a modest Franco-Ontarian town as my own?

First, the eighteen men who first gathered at St-Charles church to launch it had one main objective in mind: they wanted to get French Canadians into important positions within the federal public service. There, they believed, resided the real power, since bureaucrats were by nature survivors, and the central government would always be there. If French-Canadian children were to have a chance to prosper at all, the government was the place to start. To a very large extent, the founders of La Patente succeeded beyond their own expectations.

Ottawa was also considered to be the first line of defence against assimilation, since the fights within Québec had, for the most part, already been won, thanks to the sheer size of the French majority.

In 1966, as I sat on the small front porch of 241 John Street with my father late one starry, urban night, as we often used to do, I couldn't have guessed what he was about to reveal to me.

He wasn't a man of many words at the best of times, perhaps because he had to share them with seven children. And this may have been the first "serious" conversation we'd ever had. It was certainly the first time I heard that for the previous fifteen years he had been a member of a secret organization whose main goal was to promote French-Canadian rights. He thought that maybe I, and some of my friends, would be interested in forming a "cell" to join the cause.

He told me, chuckling, that their secret order even had a federal charter to make it all legitimate and an official publication called *L'Emerillon* (named after Jacques Cartier's ship). Covert operations ranged from influencing politicians on pro-francophone policies to taking control of institutions such as school boards and "caisse populaire," or "credit union" boards, from putting promising French-Canadian students through university to buying up houses in French communities and making sure a francophone family would live there. The members were or quickly became fanatical about "la cause," blindly obeyed the orders of "La Chancellerie," and surreptitiously infiltrated any organization that could be useful in achieving their ultimate goal: the survival and promotion of the French-Canadian and Catholic race. Local elections inevitably prompted secret meetings of "La Patente" where a list of favoured candidates would be drawn up, when they didn't draft one of their own members. The secrecy made them dangerously effective when public debate would have backfired against such militants. He mentioned that there might be some things I would have difficulty living with — mainly the religious part of it — but that it was still worth considering.

I asked him what on earth this secret resistance organization had ever done. I hadn't seen anybody blow up telephone poles or anything like that. He replied that, among other things, the Order was largely responsible for the adoption of the new Canadian flag.

In fact, La Patente had for years had its own version of what it thought should replace the despised Red Ensign. I had seen it flying over a gas station on Montreal Road, a red and white flag split by a diagonal line with a green maple leaf in the middle.

"That was our flag," said my father, smiling. We ended up, of course, with the current red and white maple leaf, which dangerously resembles it.

For some reason, earlier childhood questions came back to me, and I remembered having asked my father what that flag was years before. He had answered simply it was what he hoped would one day fly over Canada.

He also said something about the official bilingualism policy, which, although already hotly debated, was not to come into force until two or three years later. Discovering, as a fourteen-year-old, that my father was a resistance fighter not only produced a shock to the system, but filled me with a great sense of pride and destiny.

To this day, former members of La Patente are often reluctant to discuss their deeds. And it was only when he found out I was writing this book that Jean-Jacques

Gratton admitted to me that, back in 1955, not only was he a member of the Order, he was "Grand Commandeur" — the leader — of his parish.

The parishes were known within the Order by the code "xc," whereas the top brass, "La Chancellerie," was the "cx." "We were the doers," explained my father. "The cx gave the orders and they filtered down through the system." Doers' activities in this case were closer to being "dirty tricks."

To give you an idea of how big La Patente had become in those days, let's just say that in my father's parish of St-Esprit (St-Charles had been split by then), which contained seven hundred families, it had fifty-five members. When you consider that only males were admitted, which meant really only the heads of households, you can only imagine how such numbers could multiply throughout French parishes in Ontario, Québec, New Brunswick, and the rest of the country.

"In fact that was part of our downfall," says my father. "We didn't need that many people to do what we had to do. But the cx told us to recruit and recruit, so we did. . . . And people started to talk. It was bound to blow up."

The tactics of La Patente were rather simple in their design and have a definite autocratic-church feel to them. In French, it is called "noyautage," the best translation of the word being "infiltration and control." They recruited the "best members" of the community to use both their influence and their money to take over targeted organizations. Usually, these were local authorities, like city council or a *caisse populaire*. "We controlled the *caisse* so thoroughly," says my father, "I think every member of the board was also in La Patente." *Caisses populaires*, though financial institutions, were yet another creation of the church, although they have now evolved into big business giants. Most, if not all, had names that referred to their parish of origin, as in "St-Charles," "Ste-Anne," or "Notre-Dame-de-Lourdes." Many of these names have now been laicized.

In such an environment it seemed only natural that virtually all the separate schools were also controlled by the church. Which explains how, starting in grade one, we were encouraged —if not ordered— to open an account with our *caisse populaire* at the rate of twenty-five cents a week. The teacher would collect "religiously." Since the church was the driving force behind La Patente itself, and chose its membership according to its own rules, it was a cinch to put those same members in charge of school boards and credit unions. These were elected positions, so an accident could always happen. But the recruiting of businessmen and upper-class francophones was a priority for La Patente. They had the money to make all things possible and the secret structure to impose their choices. Any derogation from the Order's commandments brought on retribution in the form of unofficial banishment from the francophone community and, possibly, the Catholic church itself. It made it more difficult to go to Heaven.

Any orders from La Chancellerie were obeyed to the letter by those who had infiltrated different organizations. Non-members of the Order were to be persuaded or influenced by friends to vote a certain way: lists were drawn up to establish who would approach a key non-member — not necessarily a francophone. These people were usually totally ignorant of the existence of La Patente and had no idea that their friend's opinion was actually dictated by an organization.

When it came to the *caisses populaires*, for instance,

their strategy, as at Notre-Dame-de-Lourdes (later to be renamed Vanier, and still later Trillium), was to take control of the board of directors. That meant La Patente could choose the bank manager and, therefore, control the money — more precisely business and mortgage loans. Francophone managers of other regular chartered banks were also highly sought-after recruits. How many transactions they arranged as a result of influence peddling is a secret only the Order's most involved members know. No records were kept of such borderline dealings, and the surviving Pieds Noirs would never reveal them. But multiply the Vanier situation by a couple of thousand and you have an idea how much control La Patente had over the French community. They didn't need a big war chest for their efforts; all they had to do was infiltrate a few banks, one parish at a time.

And they didn't need to recruit everybody in a position of power to accomplish their goals. They merely had to make sure "friends" of a given person were in a position to influence those who had the respect of the community in other areas.

For instance, members of the Order did not encourage their members to join the Knights of Columbus because it was considered an English organization with few important objectives. But they did not discourage them either, since the Knights of Columbus had a religious side. They managed to create a French version of the "Chevaliers de Christophe Colomb," and they could always find people to lean on their president or executive members when necessary. In fact, they tried to outplay the Knights of Columbus by forming the "Chevaliers de Champlain," a strictly French organization. They believed that it was the only way to attract the working-class francophones who had no desire to become heroes

43

of the race but whose numbers were still needed to win the difficult battles such as that waged over bilingualism policy. The experiment failed miserably, because that was simply not up the French church's alley.

The Order totally discouraged its members from belonging to so-called neutral clubs, such as the Lions or the Kiwanis. They had little or no control over those groups, and did not see their utility. It was a waste of time for French Canadians to "collaborate" with such organizations. There was a bigger battle to be won. Besides, eventually the elite members of the Order formed the Richelieu Clubs, still the most influential charity organization and assembly of French-Canadian business and community leaders in Canada. Léon Patenaude is quoted as saying in Raymond Laliberté's doctoral thesis on La Patente: "The people today don't know it, but the Richelieu Clubs were also the Order of Jacques Cartier; they were formed to counteract the Kiwanis clubs and others." Unfortunately, at the time the Richelieu Clubs started, they were considered too elite and pricy for most francophones. They worked, though, because they had the money to succeed.

It wasn't easy to become a member of the secret sect, not least because theoretically nobody was supposed to know about it. Even wives were not told, although my father, married to a woman liberated long before the struggle for the liberation of women began, had told my mother about it. In fact, at some point, they decided to "liberalize" the Order a little and have a "mixed" Christmas party — meaning the wives were invited. It caused quite a stir, because after a few drinks the husbands would discuss the real reason behind their commitment and some woke up the next morning with spouses telling them they were not to attend those meetings anymore.

To become a "porte-étendard" ("flag-bearer" — the lowest grade) you first had to be "chosen" by the xc as a prime candidate. "It bordered on the ridiculous," my father now feels free to say. "A so-called candidate was followed for a year. You had to figure out if he was a good husband, a good family man; if he went into bars; but especially if he went to church every Sunday and, most importantly, if he went to Communion!" The man being so scrutinized of course knew nothing about the prying eyes dissecting his character to see if he fit in with La Patente's plans.

My father, without knowing it, fit the bill perfectly on all counts. I don't think that to this day, for instance, he has ever set foot inside a tavern.

My grandfather Ovila Deschamps was an even stronger recruit though, since, from very early on in life, he was considered by many to be a saint. Ovila never told my grandmother about La Patente. He'd say simply that he was going to a church function called "Le Saint Tiers Ordre" ("The Third Order"). As my father puts it: "The real Tiers Ordre was taking place in the West End, at St-François church. So, we knew that when he left by bus, he was really going there. When he left on foot, he was going to La Patente."

My grandfather, though, was also a victim of the Order. At some point, they had decided to have him elected to the local school-board. But when the election came along, the "Grand Commandeur" of the xc picked a new candidate to replace him. He was such a sweet man that he invited the usurper to his home for supper. For him, it was simple: the church had made the right decision and he had not only to obey, but to be happy about it.

My father still cringes when he recalls that his first decision as a "Grand Commandeur" had to do with a similar situation — choosing between two of his members in a local school board election. "I had to call them both and tell one we'll back you, and the other, we won't." The one they backed won.

The founder of the Order, the *curé* Barrette, my father says, was "a despicable man. As a kid, I remember I was afraid he'd eat me!" The priest, an obviously brilliant mind, was also pompous, and liked to drive around in big cars while he administered his parish where, by chance, he personally owned a lot of real estate. As a former parishioner who also had no love for the priest told me: "He used to preach in church that French Canadians should have many children, but he wouldn't let families live in his apartment buildings. . . ."

In fact, this was one of La Patente's neatest tricks. If they could involve a real-estate owner in their group, they could control whole sections of town. When a French-Canadian family moved out of a place, the Order would make sure they were replaced with another francophone family. This was easy to do as the *curé* Barrette, who owned many houses himself, reigned very much like a French regime seigneur over his flock. "In those days," says my father, "you would have been hard-pressed to find one anglophone in St-Charles."

Once you had been cleared as a suitable candidate for the Order, you still had to go through the initiation rites. Jean Caron, a former member and long-time federal bureaucrat, recalls that "it was scary." He can compare it to the Knights of Columbus rites, since he's been a member of both organizations. "The Knights of Columbus initiation was tough, but it was on the tacky side. . . . This one was serious. They put a blindfold over your eyes, and people would speak in undertones about the greatness of the race. . . . In its own way, I guess it was pretty tacky too, but it was impressive at the time."

La Patente's initiation was referred to by an acronym: VAPDA — "Voyage au pays des ancêtres" ("Voyage to the country of the ancestors"). You can imagine what extraordinary tales were being told then, most of them inspired by the writings of authors like l'Abbé Lionel Groulx. Meetings were not a democratic affair. The Grand Commandeur and other high officers, with a guard posted at the entrance to bar any unwelcomed guests and a priest (chaplain) always present to provide moral authority, basically recited what were the orders of La Chancellerie on a given occasion. The parish cells were not expected to think for themselves, except in the choosing of the targeted local institutions they wished to control. Every member, for instance, was expected to defend the new Canadian flag in every way possible and at every level of activity. They were relentless in such pursuits and kept hammering at an issue until it was resolved. Nobody seemed to realize that the members of "La Patente" were really an army under a pyramidal line of command.

As my father explains when asked why he joined up: "Well, we had already been brainwashed. I was in the 'Jeunes Laurentiens.'" This was a youth organization largely centred on the survival of the French race and the teachings of l'Abbé Lionel Groulx, about whom more later. My father also was told it could help him in his business. "But that wasn't true," he said. "They wanted to have everything for free!" Which is one of the reasons, in fact, why his own father, Salomon, never joined. "He was a bit of a maverick. He didn't like that kind of thing," says Jean-Jacques, with a smile. The fact is, though, that refusing to join the secret order once you had been "investigated" could hurt you if they decided to boycott your commercial establishment.

The members of La Patente had a secret handshake and a secret password. The handshake was made with the index finger extended to press onto the wrist. "If the guy responded in the same way, we knew we were members. If he didn't, he probably wondered what kind of weirdo you were," my father says, laughing.

The password, though, was more intriguing: VADMA — again, an acronym, this one standing for: "Vous avez double mission . . . Antoniutti" ("You have a double mission . . . Antoniutti"). Although few of the rank and file actually knew what VADMA meant, it was a loaded password. The so-called double mission was to preserve both the French language and the religion — not necessarily in that order. As for "Antoniutti," he happened to be the Pope's ambassador to Canada in the early days of the Order and had given a speech in which he had, not surprisingly, supported French Catholicism.

In fact, the password itself was a clear indication of La Patente's direct relationship with the Vatican. Given the number of priests involved in the affair, no one should really be surprised, but for many years, for instance, Cardinal Paul-Emile Léger, recently deceased and the most famous prelate of Montréal, was considered by the French elite to be their voice in Rome. It is not clear where Cardinal Léger fits in this picture, if he was a recruited member or simply considered to be a sympathizer. But documents show he was certainly considered a friend of the Order. What that meant was that the Irish within the church in French Canada would not make unwarranted headway and gain control of the clergy that had ensured the survival of the race since the Plains of Abraham.

It also meant the church was ready to put its vast financial resources behind the francophone struggle, as the Oblates did by supporting *Le Droit* for more than seventy years. How many other such ventures were backed by the Catholic hierarchy and ordered by La Patente? One can only guess. But chances are that there are a lot more than people ever imagined possible.

The extremely close relationship between the Vatican and the French Canadians went back a long way. After the British Conquest, there were many who relied on Rome, rather than France, to help the "Canadiens" survive against the invaders and their handful of carpetbaggers.

The "double mission," though, goes hand in hand with what many French Canadians of my generation and before were told: namely, that language and faith were rigidly linked.

When I learned of La Patente, it was almost too late for me to even consider joining, since the secret order was about to explode and disappear.

The end came as a result of many things — changing times probably being the most important, with the church losing its power and influence over parishioners who went to mass less and less often, and losing members of its own order to the world of the profane. Longtime members of La Patente themselves were losing interest in its affairs and its authoritarian approach. People were no longer taking orders so easily.

The Order was also exposed in the newspapers in two back-to-back articles, in 1963 and 1964. There had been earlier public denunciations of the Order, but they didn't seem to have the impact of the last two — probably because they happened twenty years or so earlier, at a time when few were listening. The first came in *Maclean's* magazine, but didn't seem to faze "La Chancellerie" too much. The second, by journalist Roger Cyr in the now defunct weekly *La Patrie* — the piece was later expanded and published as a book — was more devastating because it named names and described a typical "Commandeur" of the Order in these words: "He is rabidly anti-semitic and anti-English, although he affirms the contrary and states he is pro-French Canadian; he encourages people to buy at home, something he doesn't always practise himself, swears by the doctrine to make the face of the province more French without worrying about making the soul of the nation more French; he applauds every project to give Canada a flag and a distinct hymn." Those were devastating words coming from a French Canadian. Cyr still maintains he had to pay for his daring writings. One of his insurance policies was cancelled after the publication of his book and he had to appeal to more sympathetic members of the Order to get reinsured. A few years later, after Cyr became an employee of the Québec government, Premier Daniel Johnson got letters from people denouncing Cyr's marital infidelities and his infidelity to the Order, suggesting that he might be just as disloyal to the government itself.

Among the names that came out in Cyr's article and afterwards were some major ones in Québec's history, including a few reporters like *Le Devoir* editorialist Pierre Vigeant, who actually led for a while the "Grande Commanderie de Montréal." Other familiar names: Jean Drapeau, mayor of Montréal, whom the Order had endorsed as a candidate for the short-lived Bloc Populaire; Jacques Parizeau, now leader of the Parti Québécois; Jacques-Yvan Morin, former top minister in the René Lévesque cabinet; Daniel Johnson and Jean-Jacques Bertrand, both former Union Nationale premiers of Québec; André Laurendeau, co-chair with Davidson Dunton of the royal commission that brought in the bilingualism policy; several federal MPS and provincial members of the Assemblée Nationale; and most French-Canadian bishops in Canada. Even those who were not considered members of the Order — Gérard Pelletier and Pierre Trudeau, for instance — had been touched by it in one way or another, as was René Lévesque under Jean Lesage when La Patente campaigned for the nationalization of electricity and the creation of Hydro-Québec.

But, although the publication of the names hurt, it was still hard to believe that such a secret society had been operating for so long without the authorities knowing or doing something about it. The fact is that the higher-ups in the Order *were* the authorities.

What eventually caused the final demise of the Order was what may have been the first real schism between Franco-Ontarians and Québécois.

As my father put it, "We didn't need to expand into Québec. We didn't need them." That statement can be challenged, though, since it is doubtful the Order would have accomplished so many of its main goals — among them the instituting of the new Canadian flag and the promotion of Québec's "fleur-de-lys" and a series of social and economic measures, including medicare and the spreading of the *caisse populaire* movement — without the clout of its Québec members.

The problem rested in the fact that, throughout its

history, the Order's power still remained in Ottawa, while membership in Québec was bigger, and the Montréal faction was demanding more and more control.

There was also a newly emerging problem in Québec — separatism. Its main champion at the time was a Hull federal public servant by the name of Marcel Chaput. The Order, even the Québec faction, was not in favour of separatism, and called Chaput on the carpet in Montréal. In his book *J'ai choisi de me battre* (*I Chose to Fight*) Chaput tells how it happened: "I almost died of indignation. The philosopher wearing a white soutane, who was to become dean of the Faculty, read the first sentence of his intervention: 'Separatism leads to disobedience and disobedience is a sin.' For ten minutes, I couldn't say a word." Chaput would eventually leave the Order, but would cause enough unrest in the group to shake up the Québec troops and make separatism a valid option for many members of La Patente.

Franco-Ontarians, a minority in their province, were trying to tell a majority what to do. The organization was bound to come apart, as it did finally in 1965 when a split of the Order on a "regional" basis was recommended — Québec, Ontario, the Maritimes, and the West. In Montréal it was replaced by the Order of Jean Talon, which was never heard of again. In Ottawa, it simply died, although years after that apparent death a friend of mine was approached by a member of La Patente at his father's funeral. The man told him not to worry about his university fees, "they" would take care of it. Who were "they"? Where was the money? Is it still somewhere out there, being administered by some mysterious sect? An acquaintance was shocked in 1991 to have a prominent Franco-Ontarian leader sign a $1,000 cheque for the promotion of a francophone event without first checking with his executive. When he was asked how he could do that, he chuckled and said: "That's La Patente money. . . ." Was he joking? I doubt it. He was with the Richelieu Clubs.

Was La Patente as vital to the French Canadians' survival as the *curé* Barrette obviously thought? Tough question. "Our reasoning," says my father, "was simple. The Orangemen were organized and they were out to get us. If they were doing it, we had to do it."

But, in retrospect today, he admits freely and courageously that "it was racist and it was almost evil. Thank God, it has changed."

Was it so bad? Raymond Laliberté's thesis contains a devastating passage on the subject. He explains how the members of the Order finally were against anything foreign that threatened its existence. It denounced suspected communists to the RCMP on a regular basis. It backed Premier Maurice Duplessis's "Loi du cadenas" ("Padlock Law") banning Jehovah's Witnesses from the province.

Quoting some revealing Patente documents, Laliberté writes that they denounced "the international semitism . . . those businessmen, but also professionals and industrialists, who, to better con the French population, change their Hebrew names to English or French" coming to Canada "by transatlantic liners from Germany and Poland." They defined the Jehovah's Witnesses as "anarchists . . . opponents of the established order that consciously or unconsciously play into the hands of the Orangemen or the communists." While these quotes come from the 1930s and 1940s, their effects must have been felt later.

But it is interesting to note that Laliberté's thesis concludes by saying that the rightful inheritor of the Ordre de Jacques Cartier is the current Parti Québécois (PQ). Of course, he doesn't include in his analysis the rabid racism expressed above. But certainly the PQ's desire to create one nation under one flag and to use "controlled ideological diffusion, that hesitates less and less to revert to folklore and the Catholic religion" sounds familiar.

If Laliberté is right, I can't help but feel the irony that, a stone's throw away from the house where I live now, on the Ontario side of the Ottawa River, is the birthplace of an idea that could eventually destroy Canada and leave me, a Franco-Ontarian, and the founders of La Patente, without a country.

LANGUAGE:
Speak "Joual," Not White

୬ ୬ ୬

LANGUAGE AND RELIGION: La Patente was obsessed with both. The strange case of "Brother Somebody" proves that all francophones have had the same obsessions, and in the case of language, they haven't always agreed, no matter how united the front they present to English Canada.

It's unlikely that most English Canadians have ever heard of "Brother Somebody," or "Frère Untel." Yet mention the name to any French Canadian aged forty or older and chances are you will see eyes light up at the remembrance of a long-lost but fond memory.

"Frère Untel" literally means "Brother Somebody," although the translation does not do justice to the beauty of the Québec jargon that created the name. To explain it as best I can, let's say it is common in French Canada to refer to someone whose name you can't remember by calling him Mr. "Untel" — something like "What's-his-name."

Frère Untel — a pen name — is important, crucial to anybody's understanding of the Quiet Revolution and Québec society today. He referred to himself as a simple brother who loved "good cognac and Oka cheese." In 1959, when he wrote his first explosive letter to André Laurendeau, the publisher of the prestigious *Le Devoir*, he was indeed a thirty-three-year-old brother in the Mariste order, and a Québec high school teacher in Alma. Laurendeau christened him to protect him against likely retaliation from his church masters and the political powers that ran the Département de l'instruction publique, as Québec's inept education department was then known. His caution would be justified in the history that followed. But that's for the next chapter.

What Frère Untel preached in his writings amounted to revolution, even anarchy, to many of his peers. So much so that there were many who believed the character had been totally invented by Laurendeau and that, if he did exist, he certainly could not be a member of a religious order.

The letters to *Le Devoir*, with Laurendeau's complicity, provoked an unprecedented controversy in Québec as Frère Untel supporters and detractors fought a battle of words that dragged on for months and touched everything that mattered.

In 1960, the mysterious brother who had taken on the mantle of a superhero to many — and a villain to others — published a book entitled *Les insolences du Frère Untel* (*The Insolent Remarks of Frère Untel*). The publisher, Jacques Hébert (a friend of Pierre Trudeau and now a senator) of Les Editions de l'Homme, anticipated a certain success when the 158-page book went on sale for $1.00 — the price of paperbacks in those days. But never did he expect to sell 125,000 copies in a society that, as Frère Untel himself put it, "had only learned to read and write two generations earlier."

As my father said when I asked him about Untel,

"Every French Canadian who could read, read that book!" This was confirmed by almost every Québécois I questioned on the matter, and it was in Québec that the book had the greatest impact. Everyone there knew about *Les insolences du Frère Untel*, although today the younger generation probably wouldn't have a clue and even Frère Untel's contemporaries seldom stop to think about how crucial his daring epistles were to the evolution of Quebec society.

To say the book was pivotal is to understate its effect. No single document, including any of the classics of Québec literature, had the impact of the good brother's diatribe. You could point to many turning-points in history to explain today's Québec, and historians and sociologists would probably skip over *Les insolences* and underline more dramatic and grandiose developments to shed some light on the "distinct society." But the fact is that, as far as language, the church, and education — the three key elements of the upheaval in Québec in the 1960s — are concerned, nothing before or after had the impact of the $1.00 book that became the anti-bible of the Quiet Revolution. Frère Untel made irreverence the order of the day, and that attitude would permeate all of Québec society for years, decades, to come.

Marcel Chaput followed in its wake with *Pourquoi je suis séparatiste* (*Why I Am a Separatist*), which sold 35,000 copies, and Pierre Vallières shook the establishment to the point of his being accused of sedition with *Les nègres blancs d'Amerique* (*White Niggers of America*). But Frère Untel had the genius to be both first and thoroughly frank. Québec society was not used to either.

Frère Untel's official religious name — at a time when brothers and nuns had to choose a name on being ordained — was Frère Pierre-Jérôme. His real name —

57

and the one he still uses today — is Jean-Paul Desbiens. Born to a rural family and one of five children in the Lac St-Jean village of Metsabetchouan, he says his parents, who were functionally illiterate, were so poor, "I had to write much of my homework under the light of an oil lamp because we couldn't afford to plug into the Saguenay Power." The Maristes Brothers paid for the education he would never have gotten otherwise, as Québec religious orders often did over the years for promising, bright students.

But it was illness that turned him into a writer-philosopher. Tuberculosis, the disease that decimated many a French-Canadian family, sent him, at age nineteen, for a prolonged stay in a sanatorium where, he writes, "I met real French Canadians." The experience made him reflect on the current state of the French-Canadian nation and its future.

When he put his thoughts down on paper more than a decade later, they caught fire.

Frère Untel first addressed the issue of the French language, and, as you will see, his stinging words still echo loudly more than thirty years later.

He credits André Laurendeau with inventing the word "joual," but no doubt it was the mischievous brother who popularized it as he tried to shame French Canadians from what he called "the country of Québec" (back in 1960!) into trying to speak their mother tongue the way he thought it should be spoken.

Frère Untel accused the people of Québec, especially students lucky enough to get the education their parents never had, of speaking not French but "joual," which is considered by some in French circles as the equivalent of Black English Vernacular (BEV), the dialect spoken by Afro-Americans. A rich variety of English, BEV is nonetheless dismissed by some as being "inferior"; so is *joual.*

The word doesn't translate easily. Roughly it amounts to "slang," but it has a far more specifically French-Canadian meaning. "Joual" is in fact derived from the French word for horse: "cheval." "Joual" is the word an uneducated farmer, for instance, would have used to speak of his work horse. And so Laurendeau picked up on that particular distortion of the French language to highlight and define the linguistic butchery his compatriots were guilty of. Although modern linguists would not agree that *joual* is unacceptable or "ugly," the point here is that Frère Untel, like Laurendeau and other members of the Québec elite, disdained the French-Canadian language; they saw it as the ultimate symbol of a race that had wallowed in ignorance and defeat, and their view had many supporters among the insecure French-Canadian public. In the years that followed these attacks, the issue of *joual* would be hotly debated in French-Canadian society. In the 1970s many teachers claimed that condemning this slang was, in fact, a sign of a "bourgeois" attitude. Many authors would give it artistic blessing, as playwright Michel Tremblay did in his 1968 masterpiece, *Les Belles Soeurs.* But the matter is far from closed, as Québec's intelligentsia still deplores today the sad state of the French language in its schools. It is not just a matter of diction, or use of parochial words — including those derived directly from English — that is being denounced, but what is thought to be faulty sentence structure, and ignorance of syntax and grammar. Just as the debate about students' poor language abilities rages on in English Canada, so it does in French Canada, but with an added insecurity about what "real" French is. And just as in English Canada critics bemoan the fact that young people don't read, so they do in Québec.

Joual is, in fact, what an anglophone who has learned Parisian French still can't figure out after getting top marks in a Berlitz course. It explains why so many English Canadians say French Canadians "speak too fast." They may be talking fast, but they're also speaking a dialect of French that isn't taught in English-Canadian schools.

As an example, here is a true story recounted by a friend of mine who went on a pilgrimage to his long-forgotten mother country in the 1970s. He was sitting in a Paris bistro with a Québécois friend, talking away. After a while, the two men struck up a conversation with French people at the next table — in French, of course.

A few minutes into the conversation, one of the Frenchmen ask them, intrigued: "When you speak to us, you speak French. But when you talk to each other, what language do you use?"

Generally, *joual* is characterized by what the French consider to be sloppy diction: syllables are elided or slurred; sentences are sprinkled with English words, conjugated in French; and, in very casual speech, a few uniquely French-Canadian blasphemies are added along the way.

To this day, the most popular swear word in Canadian French is "esti," a *joual* distortion of "hostie," a Communion host. It is to French — our French — what "fuck" is to English. A "fucking bastard," for instance, becomes "un esti d'chien sale" — literally, "a host of a dirty dog" — in French Canada.

As many anglophones probably know by now, French Canadians generally swear by using — and distorting — religious words, "crisse" ("Christ"), "tabarnak" ("tabernacle"), and "calisse" ("chalice") being the most common. When you're really mad you use them all in one devastating swoop, as in: "Esti d'calisse de tabarnak de crisse!" That's angry.

In more puritan days, to avoid committing a mortal sin and having to confess it before taking Communion, the clever French Canadians invented what can only be called "approximate" blasphemies: "tabarnak," for instance, became "tabarnouche"; "calisse" became "caline or calique"; and so on. Such words, in our minds, did not count as a mortal sin, whereas using the Lord's name in vain did. It's not very different from anglophones who say "frig" when what they really want to say is "fuck."

Strange how we French Canadians swear with religious slurs while the other solitude abuses sex. I've often thought that swearing is a way of rebelling against things that oppress us. Sex was certainly not our problem; we may not have talked openly about it, but we had it. Our great taboo was the church, and once we revolted against it, other inhibitions went by the wayside easily. As for anglophones, well, I'll let them explain.

As for Frère Untel, here's what he had to say about Canadian French in general: "To speak 'Joual' is to speak as horses would if they hadn't chosen to be silent. . . . Our students speak 'Joual,' they write 'Joual' and do not want to speak or write otherwise. It has deteriorated to such a degree they can't even see a mistake when you point at it with your pencil. . . . It doesn't bother them. They even seem to think it's fashionable."

Frère Untel quotes one of his students who, having read about "joual" in a Laurendeau diatribe, exclaimed proudly: "We are the founders of a new language!"

"They don't see a need to change," writes Frère Untel.

"They say: 'Everybody speaks like that'. Or: 'People laugh at us if we speak differently from the others.'" This is a fact. As a child I would never have dared speak anything but *joual*. I would have been quickly classified as a "fifi" ("sissy") or somebody who was trying to speak "à la française" ("in the French way"). I remember that, even within our family, my younger brother Denis became a laughing-stock the day he came home from school and announced that, from then on, he was going to "speak well." That resolve didn't last more than half an hour after the brotherly harassment he was subjected to.

French Canadians have always been desperate to fit in. If it wasn't speaking *joual*, it was English — as long as we felt accepted within a larger group, our own or someone else's. Maybe that's what Frère Untel meant when he wrote: "We are a servile race. We had our backs broken two centuries ago and it shows."

Frère Untel quoted another one of his students who had what he described as a "diabolical objection" to speaking "good" French: "Why should we strive to speak otherwise? We understand each other."

"It isn't that easy," he writes, "for a teacher to reply to a comment like that." But he adds, after reflecting on it: "As long as you want to talk about the weather or sports, or sex, 'Joual' is amply sufficient. For primitive exchanges, a primitive language is satisfactory.

"But if you want to reach the level of human dialogue, 'Joual' is insufficient. You can paint a barn by dipping a piece of wood in lime; but painting the Mona Lisa requires more refined instruments."

Frère Untel sees *joual* as a symptom of a culture he deplores: "French Canadians — the young especially — speak Joual because they live Joual. It's rock and roll and hot dogs, parties and fast cars. Our whole civilization is Joual." You can try as hard as you want in school, but as soon as the clock strikes four, even the better students shake off this "proper" French burden and go back to their real *joual* world.

" 'Joual' is the absence of a language and the sum of our own non-existence, us French Canadians," wrote Frère Untel. " 'Joual' reflects our inability to affirm ourselves, our denial of the future, our obsession with the past. . . ."

Frère Untel's views may seem antiquated to modern linguists, but they struck a chord, and it hurt. He was the first to equate French Canadians' "bad" use of the language with the fact that they were — and acted like — a defeated people. The "enslavement" of the race was suddenly palpable, something you heard about or discussed on a daily basis, on the streets, in your living-rooms.

From denouncing *joual* it was only one step to the other common enemy. "What to do?" asked Frère Untel. "French Canadian society as a whole has given up. Our businessmen use English commercial signs and names. And look at the road signs along the highways," he wrote in 1960, with an urgency that sounds familiar more than thirty years later.

"The government sponsors night courses," he went on. "The most popular are the English courses. We never know enough English. Everybody wants to learn English. No need to have French courses, of course.

"We are a servile race, but so what? See clearly and die. Nice fate. Be right and die."

He denounced the fact that accounting, for instance, was being taught in English "in the Catholic province of Québec."

"The essential is to go to Heaven," he wrote. "It isn't French. You can save your soul in 'Joual' so . . ."

Again it hurt, because Frère Untel was the first one to dissociate religion and language, the first to underline the fact that we had been raised by the Vatican and not the mother country. An entire people had to face the fact that it had been brought up in an orphanage.

Frère Untel was not going to leave it at that. He had a solution, a drastic solution. It is perhaps not surprising to find in his words the genesis of what was to become, sixteen years later, Bill 101:

> To cure ourselves, we need strong measures. The axe! The axe! It's the axe we need to work with:
> a) absolute control over radio and TV. Speaking or writing in "Joual" is prohibited and punishable by death;
> b) the destruction, overnight, by the provincial police, of all commercial signs written in English or in "Joual";
> c) the authorization, for a period of two years, of killing on sight any bureaucrat, any minister, any teacher, any parish priest, who speaks "Joual."

Of course, Frère Untel was exaggerating for effect and humour. But the call for a revolution was clear.

And that wasn't enough, he maintained. You had to work to transform "civilization."

He pushed for the creation of a provincial language office with the argument: "Language is public property and the State has the duty to protect it. The State protects moose, trouts, and partridges. The State protects national parks, as well it should, because they are public property. Language too is public property. . . . An expression is worth a moose, a word is worth a trout."

He called for the Québec government to impose "by law the respect of the French language . . . by our businessmen, our industrialists. . . . The government should tell them: 'Get a French name and advertise in French or you don't get a licence.' We would then get rid of the Thivierge Electrique, Chicoutimi Moving, Turcotte Tire Service, Rita's Snack Bar, etc. . . ."

One hundred and twenty-five thousand copies sold. Think about it and then reflect on the developments in the years that followed. Think of Québec's constant demands for control of its cultural institutions. Think of Jean Lesage's slogan: "Maîtres chez nous" ("Masters in our own home"), of Daniel Johnson's "L'égalité ou l'indépendance" ("equality or independence"); think of Bill 101, Bill 178, and the language police. In French Canada language regulations are directly linked to the survival of the nation.

The impact of Frère Untel's writing was immeasurable: an entire society was being shamed by an ordinary little teaching brother, the power of one defying the ultimate authority of God himself, challenging the people to take on the establishment.

And they did.

The two following decades would be the most tumultuous in modern Québec and would rock a Canada that didn't understand what was happening.

Bombs exploded in federal mail boxes in a decade of FLQ terrorism that culminated in the assassination of manpower and labour minister Pierre Laporte, the kidnapping of British diplomat James Cross, and the imposition of the War Measures Act. Jean-Jacques Bertrand's Union Nationale government (the last in

Québec history) tried to deal with the language problem with Bill 63. The first failed attempt at regulating the use of French, it was seen as providing too much protection for English. Riots erupted. In the Montréal suburb of St-Léonard, Italian immigrants and French Canadians were fighting in the streets. Immigrants had been singled out as one of the main problems because they preferred to send their children to English rather than French schools and were thus threatening to upset the numbers that gave francophones the majority in the province. If you couldn't deal with the English establishment, at the very least, the nationalists preached, you could impose the respect of the French language on new Québécois.

Riots greeted the visit of Queen Elizabeth II to Québec City in October 1964 and degenerated in what would become known as the "samedi de la matraque" ("billy-club Saturday") and the St-Jean Baptiste parade was disrupted by the bottle-throwing riots on June 24, 1968, in front of Montréal's City Hall. Québec was burning, and by the end of the turbulent 1960s, separatism had quickly gone from being a fringe ideology to become a feasible option.

All in the name of language, a language we hadn't even mastered, according to Frère Untel.

After Jean-Jacques Bertrand's dismal attempt with Bill 63, a young and inexperienced Robert Bourassa tried to solve the problem with Bill 22, which imposed, among other things, entry tests for children who wanted to attend English schools.

It was a fight Bourassa couldn't win. Only René Lévesque could be trusted to settle the language issue. Why? Because the Parti Québécois had become the only political force radical enough to make drastic changes without concessions to the English minority, and credible enough to be trusted by a population who believed the traditional parties to be too linked to the still-powerful English minority.

In the midst of the debate on Bill 22, fifteen years after Frère Untel's call to arms, another media shock wave rocked Québec. This time it came in the form of a series of articles that ran on the front page of Montréal's *La Presse* from April 5 to 12, 1975.

Lysiane Gagnon, who was subsequently to become one of the most influential columnists in the province — now published in English too, in the *Globe and Mail* — wrote about the tragedy of the teaching of French in the province. "Le drame de l'enseignement du français" ("The Drama of the Teaching of French") was the title of the series that opened by saying that Québec's students — even at the university level — ignored correct spelling, syntax, and elementary rules of grammar, while they gladly embraced *joual*.

The series was all the more devastating because of the explosive political context of the early 1970s, in the wake of the 1970 FLQ crisis and the emergence of the Parti Québécois as a credible political party, and the fact that it came after a major overhaul of Québec's educational system that was theoretically to have improved things. In its own way, Gagnon's series, like Frère Untel's, was a cry for radical change.

Lysiane Gagnon put the blame squarely on the back of the government, writing that, "in the final analysis, Québec's political power holders are responsible for the deterioration of the teaching of French."

She said that Bill 22 would only create more incoherence and squabbles. "This so-called 'official' language will not even have priority where the future of a society is determined, in school."

Bourassa would be trounced by René Lévesque's Parti Québécois the next year, and Bourassa would high-tail it out of the country.

The most bilingual cabinet ever elected to rule the province — starting with a premier who had practised journalism as a war correspondent for CBS — would make the language bill its number-one priority.

In fact, Bill 101 was originally called "Bill 1." It was a deliberate attempt by the Parti Québécois to create a symbol, to show the people of "the country of Québec" that the clock had been turned back, the battle of the Plains of Abraham had been won after all, their struggle for survival was over, and that a new life — the one the fathers and mothers of New France would have wanted — was starting.

A procedural snag, though, prevented Bill 1 from being debated, and Bill 101, instead, had to be introduced. Par for the language obstacle course.

Among the first victims of the language legislation were the "Stop" signs on the province's street corners. They had been mostly bilingual, as in "Arrêt-Stop," but over the previous eventful years had become a prime target of nationalist vandals who made a point of spray-painting over the "Stop" that represented English domination.

In the midst of the Bill 101 debate, it was pointed out that France had decided "Stop" was perfectly acceptable, and linguists pointed out that, in fact, "Arrêt" was not the correct word. If they had to use a French word, the closest to "Stop" would have been "Halte" — except that word hadn't been in use in Québec *joual* for some time, and backing down on "Arrêt" represented a humiliating concession for a people who had abided by the word and held it up as a symbol of their revolution.

The PQ stuck with it. After all, people who couldn't speak "proper" French wouldn't know the difference anyway, would they?

René Lévesque admitted it was "shameful" for a people to have to legislate its own language, but he believed it had to be done. It was a matter of survival for a race that, as Frère Untel would have said, had been enslaved too long.

Besides, who could argue with him? In the late 1970s, none of the other Canadian provinces was officially bilingual or offered a decent education system to the French minority. Québec's English minority, even with Bill 101, was still far ahead of francophone minorities in other provinces. Ottawa was bilingual — in name at least — but in the West and the redneck belt of Ontario, people were still complaining about the French on their cereal boxes.

The Liberal Trudeau government had been torn apart two years earlier, in 1974, by the air controllers' language debate that pitted Québec's "gens de l'air" against their English colleagues. Trudeau friend and minister Jean Marchand had resigned from the cabinet over the issue. Bilingualism was proving to be far from the panacea that was to cure the country's linguistic ills.

The backlash in English Canada only served the separatists' cause, since they could point to the menace of assimilation and English oppression to justify their case.

Besides, Québec nationalists didn't want bilingualism — certainly not in their province anyway. It was all right for the PQ ministers to be perfectly bilingual — the people, the young especially, had to learn French first.

On the issue of bilingualism, as in its politics with Lévesque and Trudeau, Québec was in fact dealing from the top and the bottom of the deck at the same time. As long as the province was part of Canada, no one could touch the official-languages policy. Meanwhile, within its own borders, Québec claimed the right, the moral duty, to protect the French language.

The nationalists didn't care much about those anglophones who were trying to bridge the linguistic gap by sending their children in droves to French-immersion schools. The anglophones, in many cases, saw it as a gesture of good faith; the separatists shrugged. As a "sovereignist" — a softer version of "separatist," invented in Quebec — friend of mine informed an English parent from Ontario who was telling him about his children learning French: "Good for them."

That, of course, was not the attitude of francophones living as minorities outside Québec. Bilingualism was, especially in the case of the Franco-Ontarians, their last chance to survive.

In 1977, my newspaper, Ottawa's French daily *Le Droit*, sent me across Ontario to investigate the state of francophones and their language in the province's French communities.

It was a five-month assignment, the toughest of my career. When it was over, I had criss-crossed the province from Hearst to the Far North, to Windsor, at the southernmost tip of Canada, and produced a series of forty articles. My assignment was to avoid "speaking only to the elite" and to "go in the taverns" to talk to people.

Try it some time. Walk into a tavern across from the mill in Iroquois Falls and ask the patrons what they think of the French language. I was lucky I didn't get shot — by Franco-Ontarians.

Anglophones should understand one thing: Except for a vocal and fighting minority within the minority, Franco-Ontarians are not very proud to be what they are — especially the young. If Québécois speak French in the classroom and *joual* in the school yard, in Ontario they speak French in the classroom and English outside and at home.

Many Franco-Ontarians deny their French roots by defining themselves as "bilingual." This is very much in reaction to what they consider to be the excesses of the Québécois, whose demands can only cause trouble for them — as demonstrated in Sault Ste. Marie and other Ontario municipalities who staunchly refuse to provide services in French. Many Franco-Ontarians, even among the intelligentsia, are of the opinion that it's easy for Québécois to ask for everything. They don't know what it is to fight for their rights. Francophones in Ontario, as elsewhere outside Québec, have the scars to prove they do know. But that paradoxically has developed in many of them a sense of alienation towards their Québec brothers and sisters.

In Hawkesbury, Ontario, for instance, a municipality with a population that is more than 80 per cent French, on the Québec border, just sixty miles from Montréal, you can hear French spoken everywhere on the streets. Yet, ask people what their mother tongue is and most of them will probably answer you as they answered me: "I am bilingual."

Frère Untel thinks such people have had "their backs broken." He would really have been upset if he'd come on the same magical mystery tour I went on.

Take Penetanguishene, on the shores of Georgian Bay, for instance. In the telephone book, most of the names are clearly of French descent. Yet bilingualism is uncommon here, let alone French, which no one dares speak on the street.

I don't blame them. Just before I passed through there in 1977, a seventeen-year-old girl had gone through an experience that says it all. She was a candidate for president of the local "bilingual" high school and gave a small part of her speech in French. Afterwards, a fellow student — anglophone — literally spat on her because of it. French teachers in the school were being harassed by the English students with veiled threats and abusive comments about their promotion of the francophone cause, and were not really protected by their superiors.

I met the teachers — they were terrified. Of what? I'm not too sure. They just didn't feel safe as francophones in this town. I met the girl. She seemed to take it in stride. But I was shocked to find that, when she spoke French, she did so with a heavy English accent. When I pointed it out to her, she was astonished to hear such a thing. She had no idea. This was the kind of French she spoke at home. I then realized that every "bilingual" local person I met under the age of forty spoke French the same way. It's like this in every so-called French community in southern Ontario. Urbanization has totally absorbed what used to be homogeneous Franco-Ontarian communities. French for those who still call themselves francophones is paradoxically a token language. Those who want to preserve it don't stay.

As an old bartender in Penetanguishene told me when I asked him why the francophones didn't protest more: "When a cat has been burned by hot water, he is afraid of cold water." Their backs broken . . .

In Welland, I was sent to a supposedly French club to meet with local francophones. When I walked in, all I could hear in the place was English. I struck up a conversation with the bartender. He was a Québécois who had left the province to escape what he saw as the tyranny of the separatist PQ. He couldn't say enough about how proud he was that his children spoke perfect English — something he could never do.

While we chatted, one of the men at a nearby table overheard the conversation and started shouting in French: "Hey! Did Lévesque send you here?" I went over to talk to him. He couldn't care less about the French he spoke, or his French origins. Neither did his francophone — sorry, bilingual — buddies.

The situation is not as desperate in Northern Ontario, where francophones still provide a good part of the blue-collar labour force. But the miners know you speak "white" on the job. After all, many of them saw the sign at the entrance of the mine in Timmins that read: "No French Spoken Beyond This Point." Why? Apparently the bosses were afraid the workers could be conniving to steal gold.

The wood industry has protected many francophones in Northern Ontario against assimilation, for two reasons. First, a good part of it is controlled by francophone entrepreneurs and, more important, it is carried out in remote areas, far from the city, where English would gobble up the French.

In Toronto, where ethnic groups like the Italians and the Chinese are more important than the other "founding people" — in numbers and in recognition — you hear more French spoken these days, by migrant Québec workers in the service industries, European immigrants, and tourists from Québec. But as a francophone

Torontonian woman — a European — told me: "It's like a pregnant woman. She sees every other pregnant woman on the street."

French is all right on the streets of Toronto because it's not threatening. It's even kind of, well, cosmopolitan — and God knows how Toronto likes that status.

Other than some northern communities, only Ottawa and eastern Ontario can be considered relatively safe havens for true Franco-Ontarians, because of the federal government presence and Québec's proximity.

But even Ottawa did not have the bilingual image it has today more than twenty-five years ago. And even then, the citizens of Ottawa sometimes have second thoughts, as they did in 1990 when some members of City Council considered cutting back on bilingual services at City Hall.

Mind you, it wouldn't hurt much. Few Franco-Ontarians deal with the city — even in the capital — in their first language, any more than they use the French services provided for them by the province. It is a reflex that goes hand in hand with a minority that, in the end, does not want to rock the boat too much for fear they may be forced to walk the plank. Or, it's the all-too-typical reaction of French Canadians who would rather speak English than deal in French with somebody who seems to labour in the language.

The answer is as Franco-Ontarian as you can get. Most people don't want to waste time if English will do, or worse, they don't want to feel embarrassed if the answer is: "Sorry, I don't speak French."

Often, in a store or a taxi or on the phone, two francophones will speak to each other in English, even though each of them knows the other speaks French better. I know. I've done it. And I've also switched to

French after noticing a particularly obvious accent, only to find that the other person would persevere in bad English, simply refusing to be humbled into revealing his true French identity.

I understand the phenomenon. It angers me, but I understand it. I know what it is to be subjected to ridicule because you pronounce "the" like "de." I know the "CH" on the Canadiens hockey sweater means "Centre Hice." I practised consciously for years to get rid of my accent after a francophone — oops, bilingual — girl from Port Colborne laughed at my English in university.

It's the result of a need to belong, a collective inferiority complex, an inbred fear of being rejected if people find out who we really are. It's not easy when you're a French Canadian outside Québec and the English don't think you are one of them.

Many Franco-Ontarian parents abdicated because of this agony, and sent their children to English schools to spare them the suffering their parents had experienced. Today, those children can't speak a word of French and, in places like Ottawa, are economically disadvantaged because they don't speak French. That's assimilation!

Still, things have changed, at least in some places. First, in Ottawa, French is now an accepted part of the scenery, on billboards and signs. You find more and more anglophones with whom you can carry on a normal conversation in French, without feeling that you have to revert to English.

My three daughters, aged fourteen, twelve, and eleven, are fluently bilingual and speak better French and English than I did at their age. There are still traces of *joual*, and the odd English word will find its way into a French sentence, but the quality of their language is, I think, higher than mine was. It is no longer shameful to speak "proper" French.

Nonetheless, this doesn't stop the process of assimilation. Earlier this year a study in Ontario stunned francophone teachers when they realized almost half their students spoke English as a first language at home. I could have told them that.

But linguistic elites are no different from other snobs. They are blind to real life, oblivious of the struggle of the miner in Sudbury or the businessman in Penetanguishene. It's easy to be French when that's what you teach. It's easy to defend francophone rights when you work for a French newspaper or Radio-Canada. It's easy to look down from your pulpit at the "vendus" when you preach in a solidly French parish.

The Franco-Ontarians who call themselves a "people," as I heard it said at a huge Richelieu Clubs gathering in Ottawa last year, forget easily also that they owe a big "Merci" to Québec. On their own, without Québec's political clout, René Lévesque would have been right to say, as he did, that they were just "lukewarm cadavers."

On the other hand, the separatists forget too easily that, in the battle for French rights, Franco-Ontarians have been their last line of defence, the buffer zone between English Canada and their provincial borders, as are the Acadians to the east.

The Acadians. Poor Acadians. The forgotten, the deported, the brave who came back. Even the Québécois don't know what to make of them. They speak French with that strange "Cajun" accent. Franco-Ontarians are just Québécois who settled on the other side of the Ottawa River. And, in New Brunswick, the people from the "Madawaska Republic," to the north, are just transplanted Québécois. But the Acadians are an object of curiosity for everybody. They claim to be different, and they are. A people with its own history, as painful and depressing as it may be, its own literature and folklore — and yes, its own language. It is French . . . or is it Acadian? How else can it be when you can use a plural to talk about yourself in the first person and sound perfectly normal?

Francophones outside Québec formed an association few people — including politicians — listen to anymore, in the mid-1970s. Their first report was called "The Inheritors of Lord Durham." The title referred to Lord John George Lambton, 1st Earl of Durham, the first sociological expert to study the language problem in Canada. In 1840 Durham said in his report following the rebellions in Lower and Upper Canada that the best solution for French Canadians was assimilation. He wrote: "I should indeed be surprised if the more reflecting part of the French Canadians entertain at present any hope of continuing to preserve their nationality. Much as they struggle against it, it is obvious that the process of assimilation to English habits is already commencing. The English language is gaining ground as the language of the rich and of the employers of labour naturally will."

That was 152 years ago. In his impressive work *The French Canadians 1760–1945*, American historian Mason Wade writes: "The national pride was injured by Durham's frank indictment, and one of the unforeseen consequences of the Report was a strengthening of the instinct of national survival and the creation of more vigorous opposition to assimilative influences."

Wade was right. French Canadians owe Lord Durham a big one. His call for assimilation, which seemed perfectly normal and logical in the context of European imperialism, became the rallying cry for those community leaders who might otherwise have given up on the nation. Durham said we were dead, or at least dying. Proving him wrong became the driving force of a nation who still believed, in 1840, that the land of Canada was theirs and not the invaders'.

One hundred and forty years later, the survival of the French language would become the ultimate goal, when French Canadians would suddenly and collectively abandon their Catholic heritage to find a new religion in the language they spoke.

THE CHURCH:
Ite Missa Est

ɷ   ɷ   ɷ

IT WAS OCTOBER 1966. The Catholic church in Québec had already been drawn into the province's Quiet Revolution and was bursting at the seams. Although the disaffection with the church would be less strident in the rest of French Canada, francophones everywhere would soon follow the lead of the Québécois and abandon the institutions that had led their battles and the beliefs that had been at the core of their cultural identity. As the last line of the Latin mass says, "Ite missa est" — "Go, the mass is over."

But the most devastating blow yet was about to be delivered to the French-Canadian faithful who, though more and more restless with their religious masters, were still afflicted with an unhealthy fear of God and retribution.

Until then, religion in French Canada had been largely an affair of crime and punishment. In the end, the authoritarian, condescending attitude of the Québec church — and its French-Canadian branches — would be its downfall.

And the dam, for many, finally broke that autumn

when, in a move that seemed to come out of the blue, Canada's bishops announced that Catholics could now eat meat on Fridays. Previously, transgressing this church commandment — as opposed to God's Commandments — had been classified in the mortal-sin column, which meant you went straight to Hell without passing "Go" should you die without first confessing to this horrible crime.

For my family, it meant a merciful end to macaroni, beans, and boiled eggs. My father didn't eat fish, so we rarely did.

It was hard to believe that, all of a sudden, Friday had become like any other day of the week. We, like most French-Canadian families, quickly celebrated with meat.

But after the initial euphoria, the problems began. Québec society had already been rocked by too many changes, too quickly: the Quiet Revolution had brought changes in education, political beliefs, and behaviour; the start of organized separatism; the nationalization of Hydro-Québec (a sign that the government was ready to use its money and clout to take control of the economic sector against American and English interests); and more. With changes in church ritual, a terrible nagging doubt entered the collective psyche. How could the priests who had been teaching us, blessing us, ordering us, saving us, suddenly alter the rules of the game? How could they have scolded the sinners as vehemently for eating meat on Fridays as if they had committed adultery, and now call the whole thing off?

And, if eating meat was no longer a crime, what about the rest of the rules? Meat on Friday had been for many French Canadians a symbol as important as the "Stop" signs in the language debate. Compulsory attendance at mass on Sundays was also a commandment of the church. Did the rescinding of the commandment about meat mean that it might not be a sin tomorrow to skip mass?

We'd been had — and not just the parishioners, but their priests as well. Soon the religious orders would feel the full impact of the uncertainty and confusion that had gripped the community. An alarming number of churches would soon be deserted on Sundays, and the priests themselves, feeling no longer useful in a society that had suddenly lost faith in them, would quit the vocation in droves. When they started marrying former nuns we knew our once orderly, obedient, and peaceful existence had reached the point of no return.

I continued to attend Sunday mass for a while. After all, going once a week was nothing compared to the rigours of the seminary. And, in an effort to keep up with the times, the Québec Catholic church approved what they called "messes à gogo," as in "go-go dancing." Now guitars and other diabolical instruments could replace the antiquated organ — and the old woman who thought she knew how to play it. My real start in rock and roll was on three chords and a prayer. We had a choir of sorts — a mixed choir — and we all knew why we were there: it was an easy way for boys to meet girls and vice versa. The head priest didn't like this defamation one bit, but his younger vicar convinced him these were changing times. The *curé* Baribeau wasn't too sure about that. After all, wasn't this the same music the Catholic church had denounced as coming from Hell fifteen years earlier? Wasn't it the same music they had played at the graduation balls that Montréal bishop Joseph Charbonneau wanted to ban in the late 1940s?

The new mass kept attracting people for a while. But, like everything else the church tried, like the prayers it had forced us to learn by heart, it was superficial and bound to go the way of fish on Fridays.

I could see the institution collapsing around me. Most of my friends stopped attending mass, and my younger brothers started to do the same. It saddened me at first but, pretty soon, I started to join them at the bowling alley, the most crowded place between 11:00 a.m. and noon on Sundays. And once we shook off the guilt of not going to mass, no clear link bound us to religion. Our definition of God was now less controlled by the church, more personal.

That this would happen in a family in which one uncle was a bishop and one aunt a nun is an indication of the extent to which French-Canadian society was becoming secularized. The phenomenon was not unique to Québec, but it was fundamental and as radical as, say, in a span of less than a decade, the Polish people deserting the Catholic church en masse.

From being a people who had sought refuge and solidarity in the Catholic church, suddenly we were as united in our resolve to escape it. In the words of the times, "the crucifixes went out the window," and so did many of the teachings of the church, first and foremost the virtue of patience and respect for authority. In many French Canadians' minds, if the church could be questioned, it followed that everything else could be too. It was only a small step from there to challenging the political and social order of things.

One must understand that, at this juncture, French Canada was by and large still only a "mission," in the religious sense of the word. The priests of the 1,900 French parishes of Québec still ruled absolutely over their flocks as the Jesuits who came to New France to evangelize the pagan Natives and provide religious comfort to the settlers had done.

As missionaries do, they had founded schools, universities, and hospitals; they had helped the poor; they had paid for the education of countless young minds, as they did for children of the Third World. And, as happens in a mission, they had produced home-grown priests — in such numbers that they had been steadily exporting them after they ran out of potential converts at home. The missionary priests, nuns, and brothers were, in fact, Québec's first multinational, and it should come as no surprise that international firms like Lavalin would follow in their footsteps during the boom years of the 1980s.

The Vatican had effectively ruled French-Canadian society since the British victory in 1759. The most pressing problem conquering British brigadier James Murray had to resolve in 1760 was whether or not he would let a new Catholic bishop be appointed in Québec City. The conquered settlers outnumbered the new arrivals 90,000 to 600. The British army of 1,500 could at any time have been opposed by the 9,000 Canadiens who had served in the French army. What they had conquered was not just another piece of undeveloped territory; they had vanquished a budding country. The "Canadiens," many of them born here, had no place to go. This was home. Today's problems find their genesis in that undeniable fact, and in the active role the church played in shaping French-Canadian life.

In what seems now like a familiar story, the more efforts made to deny them freedom of religion, the more French-Canadian Catholics struggled to keep their faith.

Many British settlers, carpet-baggers, and Loyalists

could not understand in those religiously sensitive days why the hateful Papists were tolerated, even given equal rights. But the British conquerors had other, bigger fish to fry. Just sixteen years after the conquest of Québec, the United States of America would declare their independence from the mother country. Less than forty years after that, in 1812, the upstarts from the south would attempt to invade Canada, and Britain would need the help — or at least the passivity — of the French Canadians to repel the invasion. They couldn't get them on side by aggravating them.

So, bit by bit, through the Catholic church, the defeated nation won back its rights, and eventually its power.

The teachings of the parish priests were crucial to French-Canadian survival. Through two centuries, deprived of immigration from France, the clergy preached what has come to be known as "la revanche des berceaux" ("the revenge of the cradles"), exhorting their parishioners to make babies, lots of babies.

In the decade following the conquest, the French Canadians attained the highest birth rate ever recorded for any white people, and the birth rate remained high until the late 1950s. The large families enslaved parents and a whole people in a constant state of poverty, but the church would provide for the education of the fittest. It was the only way to get the numbers to fight assimilation since the French well had dried up, while immigrants were flowing in from the English victors' side. It was commonplace for some children to die young. Almost every large family had at least one such death to record, usually a child lost to pneumonia, flu complications, or tuberculosis. Doctors were rare and they cost money few people had. But the church was the ultimate comfort; the children would go to Heaven and we would pray for the dead every night.

In a bizarre twist of fate, more than two hundred years later, the Québec government, under Robert Bourassa, faced with an alarming decline in the birth rate, would bribe Québécois into making more babies by offering parents special subsidies for every new child. What the priests got by bartering eternal peace, the government was reduced to buying.

All this to say that, in the aftermath of the Plains of Abraham, it was the Catholic church that pulled the French settlers up by their bootstraps and kept them going. Without the priests, there is no doubt in my mind, the settlers would have given up. After all, the British invaders, for all their faults, were bringing with them a political system much less oppressive than the feudal regime of New France — and one that would soon be toppled in France too, in one of the bloodiest revolutions in human history.

As I pointed out earlier, the priests were, in fact, missionaries, people trained not to give up easily, people who had suffered martyrdom in many countries of the world to spread the faith. That mentality would prevail for a long time as the French Canadians struggled out of their ignorance and their poverty and left the family farms and the lumber camps to find more misery in the city. It was still prevalent when the Quiet Revolution came along, and the archdiocese of Montréal was still considered by the international clergy to be one of the toughest in the world. French Montréalais were, by and large, poor refugees from the rural areas. Crime was rampant, as Jean Drapeau's campaign to clean up the city would show in the 1950s. Many French Montréalais were Catholics in name only and showed contempt for

God (they swore a lot) and his priests. They were a largely ignorant flock. The church's self-imposed task of ensuring the survival of the nation as a whole, and not merely promoting its religious beliefs, made the task even more complex and arduous. The Cardinal had to be involved in every aspect of life: politics, education, and social programs, as well as religion.

In this respect, it is impossible to dissociate the upheaval of Québec society three decades ago from the influence of the man who was known as the Prince of the Church — Cardinal Paul-Emile Léger, Archbishop of Montréal from 1950 to 1967. It was seen as excessive in largely agnostic Québec when Montréal's *La Presse* devoted its entire front page to Cardinal Léger's death at age eighty-seven in 1991 — especially since he had left the province to go help Africa's lepers almost twenty-five years before. But those who had lived through the Quiet Revolution and knew of Léger's pivotal role in the process understood fully the importance of the man who had presided over the French-Canadian church in what is still its greatest crisis ever. There has not been another towering powerful religious figure in the province since; today most Québécois would be hard-pressed to say who is Archbishop of Montréal, never mind their own.

But, in those Catholic days, everyone knew Cardinal Léger, and nothing happened without his involvement, if not his approval. His own downfall and self-imposed exile are, in fact, the most revealing examples of the dramatic extent of the changes that shook Québec society in the hairy 1960s and 1970s. He left largely because he felt that, although he could still speak out, the people weren't listening.

Paradoxically, like many reformist leaders, such as

Mikhail Gorbachev, Cardinal Léger would be, in large part, responsible for setting in motion the liberating forces that would eventually allow the people of his fiefdom to dominate their masters. In many ways, like Gorbachev, he had little choice. It was only a matter of time and, in fact, for the Catholic church in Québec the changes that came were too little, too late. The sheep were long gone when the shepherd woke up.

Paul-Emile Léger was the epitome of absolute power, of everything that was feared about the church in French Canada. He inspired obedience more than respect. He was considered a "Roman" priest, an emissary from the Vatican more than a representative of the people — the spiritual son of Pius XII, who was like a father to him; the friend of John XXIII, who confided in him; the symbol of the Pope's infallibility.

Léger was appointed Archbishop of Montréal — then the most important church position in French Canada — in 1950, in what can only be described as mysterious and unhappy circumstances. He succeeded Joseph Charbonneau, the immensely popular bishop who had made the crucial mistake of alienating Québec dictator-elect Maurice Duplessis and the church's old conservative guard the previous year by publicly supporting the striking miners of Asbestos, in what was to become one of Québec's most famous labour clashes.

Duplessis, with the help of the traditionalists in the church's hierarchy, had forced Charbonneau out of Montréal and into exile in Victoria, B.C., where he would die nine years later. Officially, Charbonneau, who suffered from diabetes, left "for health reasons." But the rumours abounded long before the truth came out that he had fallen victim to Duplessis's wrath.

Enter Paul-Emile Léger, forty-six, the young Cardinal

from the Vatican, snobbish and "triomphal" ("trium-phant"), as pompous bishops were described in those days, intimidating in his crimson regalia and gold ornaments. Léger, far from being considered the poor man's friend he would have liked to be, was seen as distant and unyielding — a sharp and disappointing contrast to Joseph Charbonneau. From a respected Québec family, he seemed destined for the same level of greatness as achieved by his younger brother Jules, then a successful Canadian diplomat, who would become, in 1973, only the second French-Canadian governor general in history.

Cardinal Léger had a direct and daily pipeline to his flock. I can still see my maternal grandparents, Ovila and Alice Deschamps, turning on the radio, every night, at 7:00, after putting away the supper dishes, to kneel and say the rosary while the Cardinal led the way. By the end of his mandate, Léger himself would become bored with the routine as the fifteen-minute repetitive sequences of "Ave Maria" and the "Pater Noster" became less and less relevant in troubled times.

The rosary that was believed to save souls was headed, like many prayers learned by heart, for swift extinction in Québec, and twenty-five years after Léger's departure hadn't made a come-back and didn't appear to be poised for one. Léger knew this, as he had witnessed and been part of the social revolution that had turned his children away from, if not against, him.

Trouble really started for him, as it had for so many others in Québec, with Frère Untel.

Cardinal Léger wasn't overly concerned when the brother sent his first incendiary letter to *Le Devoir* in 1959. Like many, he wasn't convinced he was dealing with a real man of the cloth, and after all, in the beginning, Frère Untel's letters dealt only with the sorry state of the French language and the education system.

The problem was that the publication of the first letter started an unexpected avalanche of responses from teachers from other religious orders who all begged to remain anonymous. "Why this fear?" wrote editorialist André Laurendeau.

On April 30, 1960, Frère Untel answered the question by writing: "It's simple. We are afraid of authority."

Léger hit the roof when he read: "Can you imagine a labourer or a doctor getting up in a cathedral to have a discussion with his bishop? That would be to assume that the labourer or the doctor were interested, viscerally interested, in what the bishop had to say. It would also be to assume that the constable didn't have time to intervene. And it would be to assume, finally, on the part of those in a position of authority, a respect for mankind we are not accustomed to."

"He's going too far!" Léger is reported to have said, according to a 1986 biography of him, *Dans la tempête (In the Storm)*, by journalist Micheline Lachance. He didn't mind too much that Frère Untel made fun of the clergy's outmoded dress or that he mocked the idiotic names brothers had to adopt when they joined the church hierarchy. "But when he takes all the bishops in Québec, puts them in one bag, throws them in the St. Lawrence, that's too much!"

Not only was Frère Untel insolent, but he seemed to have an incredibly strong following within the clergy itself. *Le Devoir* at some point even published a letter from a nun, christened Sister Unetelle, who endorsed his criticisms and expanded them. She denounced the oppressive conditions she lived in at her convent, how her superiors were probably worse than Frère Untel's in their tyranny over the rank and file, how a nun could not go anywhere in public — including confession — without being accompanied by another nun.

The hunt for Frère Untel was on. Within the Catholic power structure, the order was given: Find him! It didn't take them very long. Frère Untel was Brother Pierre-Jérôme, one Jean-Paul Desbiens, a Mariste Brother from Alma, a small town north of the Saguenay capital of Chicoutimi.

The Bishop of Chicoutimi, Georges Melançon, had said earlier: "If I knew he was in my diocese I would expel him!"

The whole affair took on international proportions when word leaked out that Frère Untel's diatribe would be published in a book. The head of the Mariste Order descended from Rome to censure his underling with a stern warning and a prohibition against writing for public consumption. The most pressing reason for his transatlantic trip was to stop the publication of the book.

Frère Untel bowed to the demand and sheepishly asked that the book be stopped, but publisher Jacques Hébert refused, claiming he had already invested too much money in the work. As we have seen, the book was published as Hébert had planned on September 6, 1960, back-to-school day. It sold 10,000 copies in a couple of days.

That's when Paul-Emile Léger decided it was time for his own brand of diplomacy.

"Brother Pierre-Jérôme, get dressed! The Cardinal is expecting you!" This, according to Lachance's biography, is how Jean-Paul Desbiens learned that the mighty cleric from Montréal had a word or two to say to Frère Untel.

"Eminence," Frère Untel is reported to have told his

Prince, "you are not enough of a French Canadian. You're not one of us." There are some who believe that Léger, with his sophisticated air, might have been insulted if the brother had told him the contrary. Nevertheless, nobody in those days — except perhaps the dreaded Communists — used that kind of tone with a Cardinal.

And he didn't stop there. Frère Untel told Léger that his book was his way of getting even for his illiterate, untrained father, who had had to remain quiet and obedient all his life in order not to lose the little he had. If the authorities were worried about what he thought and dared to write, where were they when his father and others like him were being exploited?

A shaken Léger asked him simply if he still remained faithful to the church. When Frère Untel answered affirmatively, Léger agreed to lift the censorship and even let the author appear on CBC television with famous Québec journalist Judith Jasmin. When it was confirmed for all to see that Frère Untel was not an invention of André Laurendeau and that he had the guts to not only question his religious leaders but confront them before the camera, the literary success was unprecedented and never to be equalled in Québec.

Cardinal Léger had himself opened the floodgates.

Frère Untel then went too far, according to the more traditionalist elements of the church, by accepting the first "Prix de la liberté" ("Liberty Prize") given by the director of the revolutionary magazine Cité Libre, Gérard Pelletier (later to become editor of La Presse and then prestigious minister in Lester Pearson's and Pierre Trudeau's cabinets).

This time, Frère Untel was not only censored directly by Rome but ordered out of the country. For three years, he lived and worked in exile, in Switzerland and Italy. He returned, with the Vatican's approval, to work in the education field for the Québec government. There are worse prisons. But French-Canadian society had just found a new martyr. And this time, the church was the torturer, not the victim. Some switch, 325 years after the Jesuit "Saints Martyrs Canadiens" were killed by the Iroquois. The church had become the bad guy, the oppressor, and it was going to succumb to the spirit it had taught its own French-Canadian pupils: resistance and revenge.

Although the priests preached obedience and forgiveness, their religion didn't seem to practise it. The priests wanted us to obey their rules only and resist the rest; and everything about religion had to do with God's revenge against the wicked.

Cité Libre was another one of the Cardinal's constant headaches. Although its circulation remained small and its writings were addressed strictly to intellectuals, the magazine's impact was widely felt. The church and the conservative establishment in the province wanted the publication put on the "Index," which would mean it was officially considered unfit literature for Catholics, a sin to read.

Among those who regularly contributed to *Cité Libre* was Pierre Elliott Trudeau. In January 1950, the thirty-one-year-old Trudeau wrote: "We are educated to have the reflexes of slaves in the face of the accepted authority. We must ourselves become the authority again and let the disciplinary prefects [seminary priests] and the police officers return to their role of servants. Prime ministers hold no divine right, neither do the bishops; they have authority over us only if we want it."

Strange words coming from the man who would, twenty years later, impose the War Measures Act on his own people. As he once said: "Only imbeciles do not change their minds."

The Cardinal surprisingly decided to meet face to face with the "Cité libristes" — Pelletier; Trudeau; and Jacques Hébert, of Frère Untel fame. He got an earful from Pelletier, even though to this day Pelletier, like Trudeau, remains a fervent Catholic. The editor told the Cardinal that French-Canadian society must liberate itself from the authority of the church as a child must let go of its mother's apron strings.

Pelletier, like Claude Ryan, who was to be appointed to Québec journalism's most coveted position as editor-in-chief of Le Devoir, believed that laymen were the equals of and not inferior to the clergy. Both, but especially Ryan, were to become confidants of the Cardinal.

Léger was starting to understand that he could no longer stop the tidal wave. These were intelligent men, leaders, Catholics — and, to boot, like him, all federalists. They had to be taken seriously.

Léger went to John XXIII's Vatican II ecumenical council determined to work with the progressive forces within the hierarchy, if only to save his archdiocese.

Vatican II is another all-important milestone in the Quiet Revolution. Not only were the priests and nuns shedding their robes to look more like ordinary human beings — although somehow, to a trained Catholic eye, they always retained an air that betrayed the camouflage — but it was now deemed acceptable to practise a religion other than Catholicism.

That was a profound change for Québec's religiously

monolithic society. Perhaps this story, told to me recently by a forty-year-old Québécois from the northern region of Abitibi, best illustrates the changes.

As a child he befriended a neighbour his own age and was getting along fine with him. "One day my mother told me: 'He's a nice boy, isn't he?' I answered: 'Yeah . . . but it's too bad, he's going to go to Hell.' She was puzzled and asked me why. 'Because he's a Protestant,' I said."

This is what we were all taught. But now it was all right to be different. It didn't mean eternal damnation. Most of us breathed a huge sigh of relief. In our hearts, we had known all along.

Remember that this was the era of Camelot, the time of great men and bigger dreams. Those who lived through that fantastic period still long for the glory days of John XXIII, John Kennedy, Nikita Khrushchev, Fidel Castro, and Charles de Gaulle. They were dangerous but exciting times. The Cold War was at its most frigid, but the space race was on. Men and women looked at a moon that was no longer unreachable. The sky was, indeed, the limit. Youth was to take over the world as never before in its history, established ideas would collapse like so many houses of cards, and the peace-and-love hippie movement — with its drugs and sexual liberation — was just around the corner.

Québec, far from being spared, would be at the forefront of the revolution.

Cardinal Léger felt change in the air and tried to retake the initiative. For all his efforts, he ended up following his flock.

One of his most important interventions at Vatican II — where he was a prominent participant, not just an observer — had to do with sex, marriage, and "the pill."

Québec Catholics, becoming more and more daring as change challenged them to do so, had gradually turned to the newly popular method of contraception. That was fundamentally in opposition to the church's doctrine, which maintained that marriage was meant to create children, not to glorify sex.

Cardinal Léger took many by surprise when he destroyed that long-held tenet in Rome, and the progressives won out over the conservative wing. The consequences were immeasurable for Québec. Officially, the "revanche des berceaux" was over. Sex was not sinful anymore, and big families became unnecessary, or so many thought.

To Léger's regret, the council did not decide on contraception, and Pope Paul VI eventually went against "the pill." But for French-Canadian women, it was too late. Some still sought approval among the clergy, which, by then, had largely given up. The Pope's position did not have to be interpreted literally, many were told in confidence by their priests.

The church did make an effort, through pre-marital courses, to convince its disciples to use the "rhythm method." But the majority weren't convinced and opted for the easiest way out. Evidently at least one commandment did not have to be obeyed to the letter any longer.

I remember my own pre-marital course — before my first marriage, I should point out. The Catholic church had decided to make these courses compulsory in an effort to prevent its faithful's mistakes and thereby to reduce the alarming divorce rate — another Quiet Revolution phenomenon we used to think was the lot of Hollywood sinners. One of the classes was to be on sex, and I recall our group of young men and women, bursting with hormones, looking forward to something that wouldn't be as boring as the rest. When the time came, an older Catholic couple taught us about the rhythm method. Everyone was mightily pissed off. We wanted to talk about sex! Who were these people? The remnants of the old Catholic church, the last of a breed determined to hang on and give the priests a chance.

But soon even those remnants would demand greater participation in the management of church affairs. They would never go back to the traditional master-servant relationship that had existed for so long. Eventually, some chosen ones would even be made "deacons" of the church, which meant, among other things, that they could give Communion, a surrender of the priest's last prerogative.

Cardinal Léger would leave behind, in 1967, a Québec that had become too stormy even for his tortured soul. He had long cherished the dream of working with the lepers, as Jesus had done, but by many, his resignation would be seen as an abdication of his responsibilities in troubled times he could no longer cope with. Many cried, but just as many shrugged.

Before his departure, he would have to suffer one more crushing blow from l'Abbé Lionel Groulx, the sovereigntist priest who had been the conscience of French Canadians in the twentieth century.

At eighty-nine years of age and close to death, the venerable priest would write in his memoirs: "What should we think of our 'mute' episcopate — I am not the only one to think so — rather weak in great personalities, and sadly losing its influence? . . ." He accused the Québec bishops of sometimes speaking to celebrate the centenary of Confederation but being unable to "settle the matter of denominational schools" or "stop the moral debacle." He accused them of having let the government "take away our seminaries and colleges, the only recruiting-grounds of the clergy."

He went on: "I am distressed, I suppose, by the defection of too many priests and nuns who give way themselves, in too many numbers, to the sexual storm. I am just as distressed by the disappearance of the priests, brothers, and nuns from teaching and education. We are sinking slowly but surely toward intellectual mediocrity."

Finally, one parting political shot from the old stalwart: "I am still convinced that in forty, maybe even thirty or twenty-five years — history goes so fast — independence [of Québec] will become inevitable. The drama of the French Canadians is tragic: will we be able to stay within Confederation without losing our lives? Independence . . . will come from our political leaders when they are backed into dead ends." He wrote that twenty-five years ago, long before the debacle of the Meech Lake Accord. Our own Nostradamus?

More than 5.7 million Québécois and one million francophones living outside Québec still claimed to be Catholics in 1990. That is pretty close to the total French-Canadian population of the country.

It is estimated that, in Québec, some 20 per cent regularly attend mass. Most of them are assuredly like me. Even if we have abandoned the church, the Catholic culture is too strong, too much a part of our history, collective and individual, to shed entirely.

When we are asked in a census, for instance, to state our religion, most of the French Canadians I know will answer: "Catholic, but . . ." Everybody knows the "but" is loaded with meaning. It means we were born into a Catholic family but have not practised the religion in a long while. We still like to get married in the church and, following that, we still have our children christened. It's a sort of insurance, I suppose. What if the priests were right? We often send our children to Catholic schools, when that option is available, if only because we want them to choose their own destiny in the future. My children know I don't practise. They don't seem to hold it against me, although my twelve-year-old daughter did ask me why I didn't go to Communion at her Confirmation last year. I tried to say that it was a personal thing, but finally she squeezed it out of me: I do not believe. Strangely, I feel bad — perhaps guilty — that it had to come to this. How many French Canadians are like me? They would hesitate to say. Religion has become a very personal thing, a taboo. Do what you think is right, and God — if he exists — will do the rest.

The priests, for their part, are still weathering the storm. In the late 1970s and early 1980s, after the massive defections from its ranks, the Québec church radicalized itself in a style similar to that of the Latin American clergy, and espoused more social causes. Since then, through the Canadian Conference of Catholic Bishops, the Québec church has imposed its radically reformist views, defending the poor against the government and denouncing the tyranny of dictatorships around the world, especially in Latin America. Canadian Catholics have had their own Meech Lake. Within the Catholic church the two linguistic sides function separately. Since the early days of the British regime, there has always been immense distrust between the French Canadians and the Irish clergy. The Irish were viewed by many as our worst enemies before the Quiet Revolution. As we have seen, they were suspected, rightly or wrongly, of wanting to take over the direction of the church.

"You don't see that anymore at the bishops' level," says a Québec priest who is close to the Conference. "But it still exists at the level of the parishioners. . . . And we know that some anglophone bishops are anti-French. We know that." Gone, is it?

"The two clergies are very different. The anglophone bishops by and large are more 'triumphant' [that word again], authoritarian, distant, conservative. . . . The Québec bishops are much more progressive," he says, "and simpler, closer to the people. . . . We had our Quiet Revolution and the bubble burst. When the anglophones have theirs, look out. And it will come. It will burst."

The priest says the two are as different and distinct as their two societies. "The French-Canadian mentality is more analytical, asks more questions. The English are more pragmatic."

The Conference provides translation, but not at the bishops' meetings. "Translation is the worst form of colonialism," maintains the priest. "Everybody speaks his own language and is expected to understand the others." No doubt that initiative comes from the Québec representatives who still form a majority within the church.

Still, we are a long way from 1946, when some 2,000 priests were ordained in Québec. In 1989–90, in all of French Canada, only 10 new priests were ordained. In the same year 88 priests died. A sign of changing times, there were a total of 248 lay "permanent deacons" in Québec and 49 in other French parishes in the country.

All together Québec still counted some 6,400 priests, but that is still about 1,300 fewer than in 1972. In fact, there are now in all of Canada the same number of diocesan priests as there were in 1946, when the Catholic population was roughly half what it is today.

A study done in 1988 indicated that back then fewer than 10 per cent of all priests were below forty years of age. More than one-third of priests were older than sixty-five and almost 40 per cent between fifty and sixty-four years old.

If these numbers are a concern to all true Catholics of both linguistic groups, they illustrate in black and white the extent of the changes in a French-Canadian society that was totally dominated by one religion for more than three centuries before the Quiet Revolution.

The people need their opiate, however. Many are still looking. Many have found that religion in the fleur-de-lys and its message of paradise at the end of the struggle. Liberal leader and separatist-basher Jean Chrétien has often said that, in the 1970s, the Parti Québécois was "like a religion."

He is only partly right. It wasn't "like" a religion. It *was* a new one, and just as fanatical and exclusive as the old. The fleur-de-lys replaced the cross and the crucifixes. The religious hymns were abandoned for the folk-singers' call for affirmation and independence. The priests' sermons exhorting the faithful to obey God's law were traded in for a new gospel preaching the preservation of the Québécois nation at all costs and above all else. The nationalist rhetoric was as black and white as the "Little Catechism." There were few grey areas. If you were not with Québec, you were against it. Retribution would be the lot of the "vendus," those who would sell their souls to the devil of the majority. As in the church, there were moderate leaders — René Lévesque being one of them — who tried to smooth over the rougher edges — bordering on intolerance — of the new teachings, but even they were being pushed along by a more radical and unbending elite in the mould of the St-Jean Baptiste Society. "La Patente" was still alive, but out in the open, with an army of followers who were begging to be told which way to go politically, as they had longed for directions to Heaven before. The result was a movement of awesome power, as sweeping as communism in its heyday, if only because it provided simple answers for all the tough questions. Outside Québec, other French Canadians watched the procession go by, knowing it was leaving them behind.

EDUCATION:
The Enemy Within

≥∂ ≥∂ ≥∂

WHAT YOU WILL READ in the first part of this chapter may shock you. At times, I must say, it made me laugh out loud in disbelief. Yet it brought back childhood memories, vivid memories, that lay buried in the corner of my mind where I put things I'd rather forget.

To be fair, what you are about to find out — and I doubt too many non-francophones know — no longer exists in the province of Québec or, for that matter, in the French Catholic system that I had to endure outside the province.

My generation, aged thirty-five to forty-five, was the last to be subjected in school to an indoctrination so sick and inane that it is ludicrous by today's standards. If we can now scoff at it all, we can thank the enlightened francophones who preceded us, exposed it, and dared challenge a then-powerful establishment to topple a regime obsessed with purity and righteousness.

The demise of the Catholic church — the common denominator in this story — had a lot to do with it. But so does the fact that this same church was responsible for educating even a small fraction of a population that had been largely illiterate at the turn of the century and through the Depression. Those who went on to read books — even those titles blacklisted by the clergy — and expand their minds, those who dared travel abroad and learn there was a world outside Québec's suffocating atmosphere, those who wrote or spoke publicly about it later, realized the folly of it all and worked to change it.

One cannot understand the constant state of upheaval the Québec and other francophone education systems have been through without going back to what preceded it. The mistakes that were made in feeding children what can be described only as garbage have a lot to do with the fact that the world of education has been under perennial close scrutiny in Québec since the Quiet Revolution.

We are obsessed with it, because we simply do not want to repeat the past. Unfortunately, extreme situations often produce extreme reactions when a collectivity suddenly decides to break out of the shackles that have imprisoned it for too long. And so, Québécois are still far from satisfied, after three decades of revolution in their education system, that they have achieved the right balance. Schools are the highest priority, because they are the first link in the chain that creates a homogeneous society, a national will, and, with it, collective hope. Immortality is sometimes achievable through your accomplishments, but more often, through your children and their children. If the race must live, the kids have to learn that it is worth keeping alive.

In trying to save the race, the church destroyed itself because it became the oppressor. The worst part of it was not so much the excessive religiosity, which we who attended Catholic schools were forced to confuse with religion. It's the fact that we were being taught as though we were a society of morons you had to go easy on, as though we didn't have the capacity to learn any more, any other way, or at any speed but slow: rote learning was the order of the day. In the minds of the priests and their elite collaborators, education was to be, for us, like mirrors and beads for the Indians of the New World: something that wasn't worth much to the teachers, but would keep us content and malleable. It was also a not-so-clever exercise in brainwashing.

Once again, the loudest and most listened-to call for revolution came from Frère Untel, who suggested that the education department, known then as "le Département de l'Instruction publique," be literally "shut down." "I propose that we give every member of 'le Département de l'Instruction publique' every medal that exists, including the medal for agricultural merit; let us even create a few special medals, for example a medal to Solemn Mediocrity; let us provide all these people with a comfortable and well-paid retirement, and then send them back to their mothers. It would still be cheaper than to pay them to complicate our lives, as they do now. Because, in the end, the Department has more than proven its incompetence and irresponsibility."

Frère Untel called for such radical measures even though he admitted that, in Québec, in 1960, to criticize "le Département" amounted to being "anti-clerical."

He said the school authorities governed by intimidation, like the church:

> The exercise of authority in the province of Québec is equivalent to the practice of magic. In politics we have a subservient king; for the rest, we have sorcerers. They rule by fear and the mystery they build

around themselves. The more removed it is, the more mysterious; the more it hits us by surprise, the better; the more it seems to be coming directly from God, like thunder before Franklin. . . .

The failure of our education system is the result of the failure, or at least the paralysis, of thought itself. Nobody dares to think in French Canada. At least, nobody dares think too loudly . . . there is only one way never to be wrong, and that is never to search for anything; only one way not to get lost, sleep. We have invented a radical method to kill caterpillars: we cut down the trees.

There is practically no way to dissociate thought from religion. Everything is inextricably mixed up. We act like the Zulus. The profane becomes sacred: we bless bridges and restaurants and so we make the sacred profane, because we mix it up with everything. . . . If it rains two Sundays in a row, it's because women are indecent; but if it rains the day of a pilgrimage, it's because God is testing the faith of just men.

Frère Untel also went on to say that the teachers within the system "know nothing" and that they should be sent to school themselves for two years, "after which we can reopen the shop."

You will understand, after reading what follows, that teachers truly had to be either very intimidated by authority or pretty ignorant themselves to agree to fill young minds with such idiocies. You will also see that, after thirty years, things may not necessarily have changed for the better.

Two years after Frère Untel's unprecedented assault on the establishment, a couple by the name of Solange and Michel Chalvin surveyed the books that were being used to teach children in elementary schools in Québec. They published their findings in a book called *Comment on abrutit nos enfants* (*How They Make Our Children Stupid*), a collection of damning quotes from the textbooks used to teach children from grades one to seven in the Catholic school district of Montréal — where most of the educational unrest has taken place over the last three decades. Although they limited their research to that area, I recognized many of the books I was given to learn from in an Ontario elementary school. Chances are they were roughly the same in the rest of Québec and in the church-supported francophone school system outside the province.

It was not mere coincidence that the book was published only two years after Frère Untel's *Insolences* and contributed greatly to the fanning of the fires of demands for a major overhaul of the education system from Québec Liberal premier Jean Lesage.

Claiming they were Catholic parents concerned with the religious education of their children, the Chalvins denounced "a program that gives too much place to religious education where it is most reactionary and unhealthy."

They identified a list of eight evident weaknesses found in almost every textbook in use at the time: "1) an abundance of overused clichés; 2) shades of racism; 3) lyrical and false patriotism; 4) childish and obtuse language; 5) grammatical mistakes, bad and incorrect use of French, anglicisms; 6) shades of sadism and anthropomorphism; 7) chosen texts from mediocre authors (when they choose good authors they chop the original version and 'adapt' it shamefully); 8) a repetition of the same exercises and the same lessons from one grade to another."

On top of all this, they pointed out that French Montréalais went through elementary schools without learning anything about geography or natural sciences; those subjects were largely left up to the initiative of individual teachers.

Here are a few of the nuggets the Chalvins unearthed.

Consider this uniquely French-Canadian way of teaching math. First of all, Québec children were not taught mathematics before grade three in those days, and no great importance was given to the subject even once they started learning it. As a result they reached high school with only very rudimentary knowledge of arithmetic and were far behind their anglophone counterparts — as I was when I had to leave a Québec boarding-school to attend a high school in the Ontario system.

The French-Canadian pupil's grade-three math text, authored by one M. Beaudry, was called *Calcul vivant* (*Living Addition*). As the Chalvins rightly pointed out, it was hard to distinguish that book from the "Little Catechism."

At some point, to try to teach division and multiplication by two and three, M. Beaudry gives life to the "complex" operation by taking students on a visit to the St-Joseph Oratory — Montréal's famous Mount-Royal domed church. They enter, of course, like every good Catholic in those days, by the Souvenir Shop. (The most obedient and faithful climbed the countless steps on their knees.)

If they were like me when I went on a field trip with my class at age ten, their parents had probably given them money specifically to buy the tacky rosaries and religious medals on sale at the holy site. You couldn't go to the Oratory — or St-Anne-de-Beaupré or Notre-Dame-du-Cap, for that matter — without buying souvenirs that a priest would bless later.

In a section titled "Pilgrimage to the Oratory," the author asks students these tough questions:

1. I paid $0.15 for three medals of Saint-Joseph. How much does one medal cost?
2. Two illuminated holy pictures cost me $0.14. How much does one holy picture cost?
3. Three rosaries cost me $0.69. How much does one rosary cost?
4. I also bought three cases for the rosaries. I paid $0.36. How much does one case cost?
5. Four little crucifixes cost me $0.84. How much does one crucifix cost?
6. Two statues cost me $0.68. How much does one statue cost?

It must be said that, even back in 1962, the souvenir shop at the Oratory was already the object of popular ridicule, and many lay teachers were rebelling against herding students into it. But the textbooks were still in use, whereas better and more advanced programs existed in France, if the Québec government insisted that translated English texts not be used.

To students in grade five — ten years old — the author poses the problem: "To climb up a mast and install the niche for the Virgin Mary, four boy scouts took two hours . . . in general, to do the same job, would it be faster with one scout or many scouts?"

If you can figure that one out, you're a better mathematician than I ever was.

More tough questions for fifth-graders: "How many months are there in a year? What year are we in? What date is New Year's Day?" And to really throw a zinger in there: "What pious tradition must respectful children obey on that day toward their father?" (This is the traditional blessing of the family by the father, something only rarely done by most of today's French heathens.)

How about this one: "What religious order was the first to arrive in Canada?" And the next question: "How long have the Jesuits been in the country?" Well, you have to be pretty dense not to get at least the first one right.

Now for the teaching of religion itself: the catechism aimed at children of grades one and two, authored by the Sisters of the Assumption of the Holy Virgin, is an intriguing mix of syrupy, overly childish prose; plainly stupid questions; and violent images, inspiring the fear of God and treating religion like a bargain-basement affair.

The book has illustrations of Jesus being repeatedly whipped and bleeding profusely, with a cutline that reads: "His body is one huge wound."

A stern and scary warning against disobedience of the clergy: "As a little lamb follows his shepherd, far from the fangs of the big bad wolf, I will always obey the Pope, my bishop, and my parish priest. This way, despite the fury of the lying devil, I will one day be in Heaven for eternity."

And: "Who can tell us if a book really has God as its author?" Answer: "The Catholic Church."

A brilliant suggestion: "Get somebody to tell you the story of the little liar who was devoured by wolves." The "Little Catechism" also tells you how to make it easy on yourself. "Say 'Jesus' and win 300 days of indulgence . . . ," that is, 300 fewer days spent in purgatory.

Need more, you six-year-old sinners? Try this: "Jesus, my Lord, I adore you as I am here in the Sacrament of your love — 300 days if you make a genuflexion in front of the Tabernacle; 500 days if the Holy Sacrament is on display and you make the genuflexion on both knees; 300 days if you repeat the same prayer outdoors when you see a chapel or a church."

I particularly treasure this one: "300 days if you say the invocation: 'O Saint Joseph, putative father of Our Lord Jesus Christ and real husband of the Virgin Mary, pray for us.'" Putative father?

So much for early religious teachings. I will spare you the details of the books that teach the same children how to read, if only because they're so ridiculous I couldn't faithfully translate the humour, except to mention Lesson 13, entitled "The Guardian Angel."

It is the sad story of a once-pious girl named Jovette who turns twenty and can't resist the temptations of the three angels of "sloth, vanity, and prohibited pleasures." To make the point the text describes graphically how "they looked beautiful from afar, but they had hideous faces and wings that flapped like those of bats." Ah, but one night, "returning home from a dance" (the ultimate sinful act), Jovette realizes she is going to die. The story doesn't say how or why. Students are left to assume that dances kill.

In any case, there's a happy ending. Just before she dies, Jovette hears a soft flapping of wings. Her Guardian Angel comes to the rescue, and the one tear of regret she sheds weighs more before the gates of Heaven than all the sins the demons have gathered to claim her soul.

The style continues in the teaching of French itself.

The fascination with death, martyrdom, brave missionaries, and the whole Catholic way of life borders on mental disorder.

The series of textbooks, authored by the "Frères du Sacré-Coeur" ("Brothers of the Sacred Heart"), is entitled *Mon Livre de Français* (*My French Book*) and covers the last four years of the elementary course — which, in Québec, ended in grade seven.

The grade-four book has an eight-page lesson devoted to the cemetery and a full-page illustration of a hearse bringing a mother to an early grave. A few excerpts: "The funeral procession has started to move: Mrs. Leblanc is being taken to her lasting home. . . . Mr. Leblanc and his two children, Gaston and Louise, accompany the mortal remains; their faces are sad and big tears flow down their pale cheeks. . . . The mortal remains are lowered in the grave. The family is barely gone and already the grave digger has started to cover the coffin. Those poor orphans will never see their mother again."

Of course, the story is followed up by several observations and grammatical exercises. Among the questions: "What do you see in a cemetery? What's a grave, a grave digger?"

Among the suggested homework assignments: "Draw a monument."

As for the perfect French-Canadian way of life, you'd already learned in grade four about the lucky farmer who thanked God for giving him "twelve and a half" kids (remember the revenge of the cradles — and no, I never figured out where the half-child came from). Now, in grade six, you encounter the traditional French-Canadian home where everybody supposedly sang and prayed "morning, noon, and night": "Because they prayed, the work was easier, the weight wasn't as heavy to carry, sorrows were eased more quickly. . . . Wouldn't it have been nice to die among our people!"

A lesson on the priest: "This man consoles all the illnesses of the soul and the body. This man, finally, has the right to say anything. . . ."

To put a merciful end to this painful litany, the main course: racism. (Mordecai Richler, take note.) In the grade-six French textbook, the eleven-year-old pupil learned better syntax by analysing the sentence: "We reminded ourselves that the Jewish people are a deicidic people." That meant they had killed a god — as my grandfather used to tell me, they killed Christ. Where do you think he learned it?

I remember the most liberal teacher I had in elementary school showering Jews with ridicule because they, in his words, were "still waiting for the Messiah."

But the treatment reserved for them was nothing compared to what the school manuals approved by the "Département de l'Instruction publique" had to say about Native people, especially the Iroquois and the Eskimos.

In a grade-four French text, a story by Father J.C. Gélinas refers to Native people throughout as "savages." In fact, it seems there is no other name for them in every story you read in these textbooks.

The author speaks of the days of Father Brébeuf, Champlain, and Dollard des Ormeaux, when "savages were really vicious."

"But the Iroquois were certainly the worst," he writes. "Ah! If you had met them in the woods, alone, without your older brothers or your father to defend you, they would have captured you, brought you to their village, and then they would have eaten you, after making you suffer for a long time.

"Nowadays," writes the priest, "there are certain savages who capture the souls of children and drag them to hell. Do your parents fear those savages? And you?"

The narrator goes on to tell the tale of a young boy, François Hertel, who had been abducted by the Iroquois and tortured for many months. He writes a letter to a certain Father Lemoyne and tells of his right hand being burned by an Indian smoking pipe and his left thumb being cut off. The author concludes this masterpiece with the line: "Is it possible not to have a soul both great and noble, not to be good Christians when you belong to a race like ours." As opposed to the savages, I guess. In some school boards, this text was used until the mid-1960s.

A publication called *L'Elève* (*The Pupil*), with a circulation of 528,389 in Québec's schools up until the mid-1960s, gives the same "accurate" picture of the "bad Iroquois" on almost a monthly basis. The Hurons, allied with the French settlers, are considered "good Indians" who are willing to be converted to the Catholic religion. So-called Pagan Indians are said to "live in misery."

As for the "Eskimos," they are an unhappy and poor lot who can find happiness and good fortune only through the hard work of the missionaries. They have other faults too. "The Eskimo is slow; he is also often deceitful. When a child dies, they bury his toys with him. . . ."

Predictably, African blacks don't fare any better. There is a story about "Koube le Noir," an African boy who is said to be "very ignorant since he doesn't know anything about our religion and still believes in bad spirits and sorcerers.

"He [Koube] will probably convert [to Catholicism, of course] some day because numerous Canadian missionaries leave each year to go and evangelize the Infidels in Koube's country.''

As the Chalvins properly point out, so that there will be no confusion, two pages later "a true little 'Canadien'" is described: "Since he was six years old this child has always worked earnestly and successfully; the future will no doubt reward him for his laudable efforts. Paul is the joy of his parents. . . ."

As an exercise in grammar: "I obey like a negro slave; You obey like a negro slave; He obeys like a negro slave," and so on.

I'm not kidding. These were real books used to teach real French-Canadian kids until the mid-1960s.

There's more, much more, but I'm sure you get the point. Many French Canadians of my generation and the preceding one have chosen conveniently to forget all this. Some even questioned my sources when I reminded them of what used to appear in our school textbooks. The line about the Jewish people really floored them.

Yet, I'm positive most, if not all of us, suffered through exactly the same instruction. Did we believe back then that the Iroquois were evil? Of course we did. What else could we do? At every turn of a page — in French, history, reading, and religion — they were pictured as devils incarnate. Nobody ever told us about the history of the great democratic society they developed long before we did, or of Champlain's sadistic massacres, for instance, which were regarded as just retribution against a godless people.

As I mentioned at the outset, it is important to remember that it was French Québécois who blew the whistle on the church's inane teachings. It was also the francophones who rebelled massively and quickly against it.

When the call for reform in the education system came, it swept the province — and, by extension, francophone communities across the country — so quickly that even Liberal premier Jean Lesage was overtaken by events; he eventually created a Ministry of Education after repeatedly swearing (to appease the church) that he would never do so. The first changes appeared in 1965 with the advent of "polyvalentes" and "CEGEPS" (community colleges), the options system, and a major textbook overhaul.

In the end, these reforms would be a major cause of Lesage's stunning defeat in 1966, as Union Nationale leader Daniel Johnson would wage his whole campaign on the back of Arthur Tremblay, the main driving force behind the reform of education. The drastic changes in the schools weren't as popular in the rural areas as in the big city, largely because, in the small villages and parishes, the priests still had a stranglehold on their flocks and could get a lot of mileage out of saying the government was taking Jesus out of the schools.

Johnson didn't have time to turn the clock back — I doubt he could have or would have seriously tried to anyway — before he died in September 1968. And he dumped the whole ugly mess in the lap of his successor, Jean-Jacques Bertrand.

After eight years of unrest, the situation wasn't simple. Demonstrations by university students had become commonplace and were turning more and more radical as time passed and the reforms didn't come quickly enough.

While some parents were demanding a "lay" school

system, free of the religiosity that had been inflicted on them, university students in Montréal were calling for free education and blaming the clergy for blocking progress, nicknaming them the "black wall." In December 1966, the French Lay Movement organized a "teach-in" at the University of Montréal, the central debate topic being: "Has Catholicism become an obstacle to the progress of Québec?"

With the church restraints suddenly gone or seriously eroded, Québec society's growing number of rebels were then looking for new targets, like armed torpedoes with nothing left to blow up. The new objective was now solely the preservation of French and the Québec state, the new religion.

Québécois were looking for problems to solve, and the merits of the language bill Frère Untel had called for at the turn of the decade were being hotly debated, while in Ottawa Pierre Trudeau, newly elected, pushed through the Official Languages Act in a desperate late effort to ease tensions. The act became law on September 9, 1969.

It didn't work. Premier Bertrand had his hands full. He had little idea how profound the revolution was, or how to deal with it. The separatists had already found a new hero in Liberal defector René Lévesque, who had become leader of the Parti Québécois in October 1968. While FLQ bombs were going off with increasing regularity, the upheaval in the education field finally turned violent in the Montréal suburb of St-Léonard.

Mobs of Italian immigrants fought angry French-Canadian demonstrators in the streets. Immigration had now been identified as a serious menace to the French majority, since 80 per cent of almost 400,000 new Québécois — 170,000 of them Italian — traditionally preferred to send their children to English schools, where they could learn the language of the rest of North America. With the church's "revanche des berceaux" doctrine not being heeded any longer, and "the pill" ensuring that French-Canadian couples enjoyed sex before family, the birth rate had already declined to such an extent that francophones felt they were being threatened in their own province, that they were under siege by a new kind of Iroquois.

It was a rude awakening. Few French Québécois had bothered with the "other" education system over the years, which consisted mainly of Anglo-Protestant schools. They had lived in relative security inside their system, which admitted no students who did not profess their faith in Catholic beliefs, excluding, for instance, all Jews from the French system.

Suddenly, however, the numbers started to come out, and immigrants began to be considered a serious problem, particularly in the province's metropolis. Immigrants made up 25 per cent of the population in Anglo-Protestant schools and some 75 per cent in Anglo-Catholic institutions.

The volcano finally erupted in Montréal when the Catholic School Commission decided it would no longer provide English schools for St-Léonard's Italian population. Ugly riots between francophone militants and Italians broke out in the streets. Brawling became common, and a photo of a French-Canadian demonstrator being kicked by an Italian made the front page of almost every newspaper in the province, with predictable results. The nationalists exploited it to further their cause.

Premier Bertrand was totally overtaken by the events. A child of the oppressive Duplessis regime, he couldn't cope with the times, which were changing at lightning speed. In December 1968, seriously miscalculating the mood of the province, he introduced Bill 85 to protect the right of anglophones to an English education and swore to push it through before the end of the legislative session. Students protested in Québec City, breaking windows in government buildings. Bertrand grossly underestimated the problems when he stated that most of the demonstrators were punks under age sixteen and vowed to use police force against them.

Four months later, he dropped Bill 85, "due to widespread opposition." But his problems were only just beginning. They were highlighted on October 12, 1969, when Montréal's policemen and firemen went on strike, creating sixteen hours of mayhem in the city. Stores were vandalized and burglarized by unruly mobs; one QPP policeman was shot by a sniper, and a Westmount doctor was killed by a burglar. Among the targets chosen by the hoodlums were the U.S. embassy and McGill University; the former a symbol of imperialist domination; the latter the pride of Québec's anglophone population, an institution Québec nationalists claimed should be "McGill français!" Two days later, three hundred separatists marched on City Hall.

Premier Bertrand was not having much luck with Bill 63 either. On October 31, more than 20,000 students and demonstrators led by the "Mouvement pour l'intégration scolaire," which demanded that immigrants be forced to attend French schools, crippled Québec City. Police used fire hoses and tear gas to discourage the demonstrators; thirty-four people were arrested and twenty injured in the crowd that chanted separatist slogans and painted graffiti on the walls of government buildings.

The government had lost control of the issue. The

once-peaceful and obedient people of Québec had taken their "quiet" revolution to the streets, as young Americans rebelled against the draft and the Vietnam War.

Through it all, the immigrants became unwilling pawns in the war between the French majority and the Anglo-Saxon minority confronted with the fact that it could lose almost half its school population. It was strangely reminiscent of the wars between France and Britain, except immigrants rather than First Peoples were now being crushed in the middle and used to settle the score.

The Anglo-Saxons, many of whom had lived in a protective cocoon of privilege over the years, and had developed their institutions within the province — including four universities and one college — had now "discovered" the immigrants and opened their world to them in the face of French aggression. Until then, it had been simply normal to leave them to assimilate to the English world. It was far from being a marriage made in heaven.

After all, this was the same group that used to ban Jews from their exclusive country clubs and make it almost impossible for them to attend McGill University or for Jewish doctors to work in their hospitals. French Canadians may have been taught a narrow form of intolerance by the church, but on an individual basis had found more affinity with the blue-collar immigrants from Ireland, Italy, or Greece, for instance, than they had for stuffed-shirt unilingual English bosses.

In the long run, the immigrants decided to stand on their own and be courted by Québec's French politicians, including the Parti Québécois, which realized they had to be "integrated" in society and not crushed into submission. "English Canadians have, since the start of the colony, assimilated the immigrants," the Québec magazine *L'Actualité* would report in January 1992. "French Canadians have only started to do so recently."

The magazine quoted university history professor Jean-Claude Robert as saying: "We are a little people with a besieged mentality. We are afraid to open up to others and disappear if we open but the smallest breach."

The same article claimed polls showed, however, that Montréalais were a lot more tolerant of outsiders than people in the more homogeneous, less populous regions of the province.

But, once in power, the PQ made sure they passed Bill 101 before they made any serious attempt at reconciliation with the immigrant population. From 1977 on — when the language bill became law — children of immigrant parents who had not attended English schools in the province would be automatically registered in French institutions.

This would, over the years, prompt protests all Canadians have heard too much about. Almost twenty-five years after the St-Léonard riots, the problem was far from resolved: *Maclean's* magazine would attribute the growing number of English school closings in Montréal to the effects of Bill 101 and the province's immigrants' mounting desire to high-tail it out of Québec, along with many anglophones, more than 300,000 of whom are believed to have left since the mid-1970s.

A week after the *Maclean's* article appeared, though, the Bourassa government would produce an unprecedented study of the immigrant population in the province, claiming the document was an international first. The investigation followed the movements and trends among some 1,000 new Québécois aged eighteen and over and landed in Québec between July and November 1989, and attempted to dispel some of the "myths" surrounding immigrants in the French environment.

The study revealed that two out of three immigrants had found a job in the province within one year of arriving in Canada. Twelve per cent were employed after only one week on Canadian soil, and half had employment after four months in the country — the figures included those immigrants not seeking employment, such as students and retired homemakers.

Furthermore, Québec's minister of Cultural Communities and Immigration, Monique Gagnon-Tremblay, quoted another unreleased study claiming that 93 per cent of immigrants who had arrived in Québec in 1980 and 1981 were still living happily in the province — contrary to the belief that has them massively migrating to English provinces.

The main governmental preoccupation remains selective immigration, however, as 37 per cent of Québec's 40,000 annual immigrants are French-speaking, a figure considered to be "acceptable" by Bourassa's cabinet minister. Québec now has almost total control over the selection process — with the important exceptions of refugees and reunification of families, which make up more than half the annual number of immigrants — since the Mulroney government has surrendered that prerogative to the provinces in a deal that was hailed as a breakthrough by Québécois nationalists.

Yet the *Maclean's* article and Mordecai Richler's incendiary comments about Québécois xenophobia — and the indignant reaction on the part of many nationalists — show clearly that this whole mess is far from being cleaned up. Anglophones worried about school closures are asking for amendments to Bill 101. After initially seeming favourable, the Bourassa government has balked at such changes and is extremely wary of toying with Bill 101 out of fear of fuelling separatist sentiment in the province and leading to the return of the Parti Québécois. "On ne touche pas la loi 101" ("Don't touch Bill 101") is the current rallying cry.

The last thing the Liberals want is to create another Bill 63. It comes from a purely political motivation that explains their apparently intolerant attitude towards English on commercial and public signs, and the bizarre solution they found in controversial Bill 178 of permitting bilingual signs inside business but only signs in French outside — one of the main reasons for the current unrest between Québec francophones and Canada's English majority.

Ironically, the federalist government in Québec is in the same uncomfortable position successive Ontario governments have found themselves in when asked to make French an official language in the province. Bill Davis's approach of avoiding an anti-French backlash by providing more services without recognizing French officially has been followed by Liberals and, so far, New Democrats alike.

It is hypocritical, intolerant, and fundamentally not right. But it's all part and parcel of the crazy politics of this invented country we are trying to give a soul.

Yet, while they take on the anglophones and their immigrant sympathizers, French Québécois are still in a state of confusion and self-criticism within their own system. They are far from having cleaned up their own house. Almost two decades after Lysiane Gagnon's shocking revelations, they still agonize over the poor quality of written French among the province's students.

The teaching of English is in a dismal state, which led Education minister Claude Ryan, formerly of *Le Devoir*, to wonder if it shouldn't start before grade four and be more advanced. I have always been convinced French Québécois by and large — even those ultra-nationalists who refuse to speak English to anglophones, although they can — want to learn the language of North America.

I remember meeting a father from Thurso, a town some thirty-five miles from Ottawa and a ten-minute ferry ride across the Ottave River from Rockland, Ontario, who despaired at his teenage children's lack of knowledge of the other language. We had rented a cottage in Québec next to his. He overheard my daughters, the oldest of whom was then ten, speaking fluent English to anglophones and perfect French among themselves. Dismayed, he came over to ask me: "Your kids, they actually speak both languages that easily?" I tried to be gracious by saying that, in Ontario, we had little choice. He just shook his head, pointed to his own children, and bemoaned the fact that they could barely say "yes" and "no" in English. He worried about their future, as do many Québécois parents.

On the crucial issue of bilingualism, Québec's elite, save mavericks like Pierre Trudeau, have been a hypocritical lot indeed. The PQ ministers especially, who, as I pointed out earlier, formed the most bilingual cabinet the province ever had, governed very much with an attitude reminiscent of that of the Catholic clergy. They could learn English because they had the moral strength not to lose their culture, but "the masses" had to be protected against temptation. The ignorant could not be trusted to remain true Québécois.

As for education as a whole, another series of articles that ran in *La Presse* from February 29 to March 2, 1992, painted a sad picture of the results of the reforms in education. It said bluntly that the professors of tomorrow are themselves uncultured and uninformed.

Commenting on the students who enroll in a three-year university course to become the teachers of the future, Montréal Education professor Gaetan Daoust says: "The Mediterranean? They don't know where it is. If I speak to them of Graeco-Latin origins they don't know what I'm talking about. They don't read newspapers or great authors."

"General culture?" says Jacqueline Lamothe from the University of Québec in Montréal. "Everything is relative. Each generation has its culture. I have a classical formation, but that means nothing to today's students.

"They ask about Expo 67, what it was, where it was," she adds, teaching in the city that hosted the event. "The October Crisis, they're not too sure about. Generally speaking, they were born around 1970."

In 1988, says *La Presse*, the University of Québec in Trois-Rivières decided to submit 167 applicants to the Education faculty to an entry exam testing their general knowledge. According to *La Presse*, 72 per cent of the students could not name three oceans, 36 per cent believed the sun passed between the moon and the Earth during summer, and only one-half were able to correctly divide two-thirds by one-half! That's not only worrisome, it's shameful. Do they think Québec is the centre of the universe? Sadly, it probably has a lot to do with it, as we will see in the next chapter.

Students haven't fared any better in the sacred French language. One aspiring teacher tried to defend herself by saying that she didn't make too many mistakes "when she wrote on the blackboard."

This is a disaster waiting to happen since Québec will need 3,000 new teachers by the year 2000 to replace those whose age now averages forty-four.

As for those who reach higher levels of education, *L'Actualité* found that 9 per cent of French Québécois quit school at the end of grade seven, as opposed to only 2 per cent in the rest of Canada.

The enemy within, for all those reasons, is still very much alive and powerful. And, despite its perennial introspection and self-criticism, Québec's school system still hasn't emerged from the Quiet Revolution to fulfil the promise of a better future for "la nation."

Which makes Senator Arthur Tremblay, the man who largely did it all, cry: "I started from the premise that children were like me. They wanted to learn, they wanted to stay in school. We hadn't counted on what I call the 'Katmandu generation' that would prefer leaving school and travelling to faraway exotic places instead."

That is a polite explanation. The polls and studies do not necessarily bear it out.

Québec society rather gives the impression of a collectivity that is out of breath after a three-decade marathon to affirm itself. The answers no longer seem so obvious. It was easy to throw out the books of the Catholic church because their weaknesses were so evident and enormous. Yet Québécois long for the "classical" teachings of the old system. The history may have been warped, but we knew some of it. The dumbest in the class could have named three oceans by grade eight. We didn't necessarily understand Graeco-Latin origins as well as we should, but we knew what they were. We read newspapers in school, Victor Hugo, Guy de Maupassant, and, in Ontario, Shakespeare.

Somehow, in getting rid of mathematics taught by St-Joseph's Oratory, the Québécois lost their way and are finding out that, for all their resolve and pride in themselves and their accomplishments, revolutions do not happen overnight. They are writing the "How to" book as they go along. Coupled with the inner political, social, and economic tensions within the province, this makes for an educational system in a constant state of upheaval, forever questioning itself.

Ultimately, it may just create a society of Québécois who will wonder how they have come to this and why. Once again, it is not impossible to contemplate that revolutionaries of the future will demand that they go back to the starting-line, as Frère Untel did thirty years ago.

While they search for their own true identity and soul, French Québécois find no time anymore for those brothers and sisters their elites once led into battle, in other Canadian provinces. For all their obsession with self-analysis in educational matters and the bitter struggles it generated in the turbulent 1960s and 1970s, Québécois tend to forget, or simply don't know, that the toughest fights for French rights in education were and are still being fought outside their borders, in Ontario.

The battle for the right to have French children taught in their mother tongue has been a long, drawn-out one in the province where Lord Durham's ultimate solution, assimilation, has worked with devastating efficiency.

A quick lesson in history is profitable here, beginning with the adoption in 1913 by Ontario's Department of Education of "Regulation 17." "Le règlement 17" is still a symbol of a blatant anglophone attempt to subjugate the minds and hearts of Franco-Ontarians.

Regulation 17 came at a time when tensions were running high between Québec and Loyalist-dominated Ontario. The question of preserving the rights of minorities in both provinces was being debated in the House of Commons, while in Europe the threat of war with Germany was already fuelling a new debate that prompted *Le Devoir* founder Henri Bourassa to write in 1911: "It seems absurd that Canada should and ought to 'save' England and France, preserve the neutrality of Belgium, annihilate the German fleet in the North Sea, and hold Austria and Italy in check in the Mediterranean, when so much remains to be done to put her own house in order."

Needless to say, the Loyalists were not amused. Like Honoré Mercier, Louis Riel, and Louis-Hippolyte LaFontaine, Bourassa was quickly branded a traitor by English Canadians, something Québec nationalists wore like a badge of courage by the time René Lévesque — another "traitor" — came along.

Against this backdrop and growing racial tensions in Ottawa, Windsor, and Northern Ontario, where the French population had grown rapidly to 10 per cent of the province's inhabitants, the government decided to impose English as the sole language of instruction in elementary schools. To make sure the edict was respected, English Protestant inspectors were assigned to monitor Catholic schools attended by most francophones. The teaching of French was limited to one hour a day.

It didn't take long for Franco-Ontarians to react under the leadership of one Samuel Genest. I am reminded daily of Mr. Genest since I live on a Vanier street that bears his name — it causes problems for anglophone taxi drivers who can't pronounce it right.

The teachers in French schools in Ottawa refused to sign the declaration of obedience to the new law, and their students were exhorted to simply leave the school premises when the English Protestant inspectors came.

In those days, unlike now, Franco-Ontarians got a lot of support from the Québec press and politicians who saw their fight as a common struggle for survival. Bourassa, for instance, had a letter signed by eminent Québec anglophones to say that it was wrong to deprive the Ontario minority of its rights. Only a few signed, however. The Montréal business establishment who saw the French majority as more of a nuisance than anything else did little to bridge the gap between the two solitudes.

Orangeman Dr. J.W. Edwards, a Tory, claimed the French language should be "driven out of the province" of Ontario. The Irish Catholics denounced the "neo-gallicanism" of Franco-Ontarians, echoing strangely the Anglican bishop who had said that francophones were threatening to export the "France of Louis XIV" to the province. Funds to the separate-school system, although guaranteed by the constitution, were cut.

Cardinal Bégin, archbishop of Québec City, pleaded the Franco-Ontarian cause in Rome, which did nothing to calm the Irish in the province. It was rumoured then that the Irish bishops were about to endorse Regulation 17. In 1914, as English Canadians looked to the European cause overseas, Québec still had its eyes trained on the ethnic problems within the country.

Henri Bourassa caused a near riot in Ottawa, where he was taking part in a panel discussion, when a sergeant from the newly recruited Canadian army, totally dominated by anglophone officers, went on stage and tried to make him wave the Union Jack. Bourassa said he would gladly do so for liberty, but not under threat. A great mêlée ensued, with francophones in the room singing the French anthem "La Marseillaise" and a brawl erupting. Later, at the Château Laurier, where he had gone after the raucous meeting, a French-Canadian man punched out an anglophone who had insulted Bourassa.

The *Le Devoir* editor's cry became: "We have no right to abdicate by committing suicide, and committing suicide in dishonour!"

Through 1915 Bourassa eventually rallied all of Québec to the cause of Ontario's French, while English Canada "was being swept by war hysteria," claims American historian Mason Wade. Québec had contributed greatly to the War Treasury, and French-Canadian battalions were being formed to boost the morale of francophones who, until then, had been integrated into the English army. But it was the Ontario question that created much of the disillusion about the need to go to war in Québec. Why obey the orders of politicians and English generals who were trying to obliterate the race? In a refrain that sounds familiar today, though, the English never saw it coming, never understood that the racial tensions they had largely created at home were much more important for French Canadians than they had anticipated, never realized that they first had to feel patriotic at home before doing so on foreign land.

Bourassa was directly linking the persecution of Franco-Ontarians to the French Canadians' support of Canada's involvment in the war. And although he was criticized by both the clergy and the Québec press, who preached more moderation to appease the anglophones, and although the Ontario English press referred to him as "Herr Bourassa," he was becoming, in effect, the true leader and defender of the race.

In Ottawa, the "Ecole Guigues," now a heritage monument to Franco-Ontarian resistance, became the focal point of the agitation. When it was closed down by the province, two sisters, Diane and Beatrice Desloges, set up a classroom in a nearby chapel. In time, the teachers forced their way back into the Guigues school defended by an army of French-Canadian women armed with hatpins.

When I was first told the story, I believed it to be, at the very least, an exaggeration, if not a figment of some patriot's overloaded imagination. But that's exactly the way it was. Mothers with hatpins against English intolerance. The story, which has attained the status of legend among Franco-Ontarians, has been told for generations. It is our Alamo.

By 1916, there was more unrest as, in Ontario, the ordinary anglophone believed that the government of Québec was imposing the teaching of French on the English minority — which wasn't true but sounds remarkably similar to the distortions we hear today about bilingualism and even the language bill in Québec. Several prominent, tolerant anglophones tried to help the French Canadians' cause, calling on the British sense of fair play. The Ontario government pressed on undaunted, and unsuccessfully tried to impose its own teachers on the separate schools by trying to break the female barricades that were now guarding just about every French teaching establishment in the capital.

On January 31, 3,000 French students marched on Ottawa's City Hall, demanding that their teachers be paid from the tax monies that had been seized after Regulation 17. A boycott of Ontario manufacturers by

Québécois started to hit home as "Eaton's and Simpson's . . . catalogues returned unopened" to Toronto, writes Mason Wade.

The debate eventually reached the House of Commons, where Québec Tory lieutenant Ernest Lapointe, despite Prime Minister Borden's objections, introduced a motion to incite Ontario to quash Regulation 17. The argument pitted Québec's Liberals under Sir Wilfrid Laurier against Ontario Grits, and Québec Tories against their English political allies. The motion was lost, 107 to 60, as English politicians from Ontario from both parties claimed that the anti-French law was unassailable.

Francophones by then were being accused of internal aggression in time of war by the Toronto press, to which the *Montreal Star* replied that they were the ones being attacked by an intolerant Ontario government. The *Toronto News* continued to refer to the francophone population as "the ignorant French."

By the time conscription was imposed, the crisis in Franco-Ontarian schools, coupled with similar repression in the West and a growing rumour of the same in New Brunswick, had already convinced French Canadians they had no reason to heed their government's call to arms.

In the fall of 1916, the "Association d'Education" opened "bilingual" schools in Ontario to circumvent Regulation 17, but could barely pay their teachers and had to organize a fund drive to buy heating coal. The famous nationalist priest l'Abbé Lionel Groulx went to Ottawa on October 15 to fuel the effort.

He took on the struggle with typical zeal, and eventually it was up to the Pope, not politicians, to settle the matter in an injunction that appeared in the *Canadian Review* on October 24, 1918. Pope Benedict xv wrote:

The French Canadians may justly appeal to the government for suitable legislation as to the above-mentioned law [Regulation 17] and at the same time desire and seek further concessions. Such are undoubtedly that the Inspectors of their Separate Schools be Catholics, that during the first years of tuition the use of their own language should be granted for the teaching of certain subjects, chiefly and above all, of Christian doctrine; and that Catholics be allowed to establish training schools for the education of the teachers. . . . Let all priests endeavor to acquire the knowledge and use of both languages, English and French, and setting aside all prejudices, let them adopt one or the other according to the needs of the faithful.

God had spoken. He also warned French Canadians not to resort to revolt and to get the permission of their bishop for any litigation action in the matter.

The Irish bishops had to obey, albeit reluctantly, and activism within the Ontario school system came to a halt. But it wasn't until 1927 that the Merchant Report effectively put an end to Ontario's policy of oppression and assimilation through education. Curiously, that was the year "La Patente" was formed, in the Ottawa French enclave of Eastview (Vanier), where the bitter fight had been waged.

Thus, perhaps you understand the feelings of revenge that animated the founders and members of the Order of Jacques Cartier. Between militant francophones and the anglophone majority, things would never be the same. Cooperation, although now favoured by the government, was something Franco-Ontarians couldn't truly believe in because they had lost trust in the "other side." The walls were built through the Ontario school crisis and participation in the war.

That is not to say Regulation 17 didn't, in the end, have the desired effect. The majority had showed an awesome power it was not afraid to use. Many francophones were lost in the process, among them those who gave up early on and sent their children to English schools or those who simply came to the conclusion the fight couldn't be won against such incredible odds and decided to assimilate themselves to the English majority. Then there were those who lived in communities who promoted local assimilation, often through unwritten policies providing only English education to the francophone population that was still sizeable. My maternal grandmother, for instance, didn't go to school for very long, but what she did learn was in English. I always found it strange, for instance, that she counted in the English language and mixed a lot of distorted English expressions into her day-to-day language.

However, almost sixty years later, in the early 1970s, as Ontario's French braced themselves for another crisis, there were still sufficient numbers of them to once again let the anglophones show the ugly side of their intolerance.

This time it had to do with public high schools and the need to get rid of the so-called bilingual institutions that were really disguised English schools from which francophones emerged having lost much of their ancestors' language and culture.

The intolerant rhetoric of the early twentieth century had been replaced by the "economic" argument in many cases, as anglophones did not see the need to spend money on French education when things were going well as they were.

Militant francophones who led the fight were persecuted in their own communities, often by French "collaborators" who disguised their betrayal of their roots by hiding behind the Canadian flag and a bilingualism policy their anglophone "friends" could not truly believe in because what they were advocating was the gradual extinction of Franco-Ontarians.

In Cornwall, where one of the most divisive battles to get a French high school in the early 1970s took place, the owner of a local men's store, for instance, had to close down his business because he sided with the French cause and was boycotted. When I met him, four years after the painful events, he refused to talk about it and was happy just working as a bureaucrat for the federal government. He had learned his lesson and didn't want any further involvement.

As a reporter, I encountered another confrontation in 1977, when I interviewed French teachers and parents who were crushed by the fact that, although they attended francophone schools, their children were insisting on speaking English at home. They advocated a policy that would require students to speak only French on school grounds, both inside and outside the classroom. The parents revolted and gathered by the hundreds in a gymnasium filled to the rafters to hear the local school board debate the issue. The proponents of "freedom of choice" for their children were waving Canadian flags.

In Ottawa, at Charlebois High School, a few years later, the principal was vilified by parents when he insisted that students speak French outside the classroom and in the school yard. He held his ground, but suffered much abuse in the process.

If that can happen in the nation's capital's peaceful

and comfortable neighbourhood of Alta Vista, what does it say about those who are isolated in English communities?

In Windsor, I had to go out of the main urban core to find a truly French environment in some of the remaining villages with a sizeable francophone population. In St-Joachim — whose name has been so distorted by local English pronunciation that I couldn't get clear directions from anybody to get to a town they had never heard of — I went to the school yard of the elementary institution. The young kids were amazed to meet a stranger who spoke French, and they engaged in an animated conversation among themselves about it — in English.

In Hamilton, while I waited to meet with the authorities of the French high school, I didn't hear one word of French spoken in the halls, and those students who finally spoke it to their teachers did so with great difficulty and obvious discomfort.

It would be tempting to believe that things have changed since I did my depressing tour of the province some fifteen years ago. But I rather believe that, although French schools have grudgingly been accepted as a necessary evil by the English majority, the reality is that few francophones graduate from them able to read, write, and, most of all, speak French in such a way that they could successfully attend a French institution of higher education in what used to be their mother tongue.

By the way, there is only one outlet in Ontario for French high school graduates — the "bilingual" University of Ottawa. There was a movement in the early 1970s to turn it into a unilingual French institution, but the school authorities didn't dare lose the English students or the subsidies that flow with bilingualism. Technically, there is another "bilingual" university in Sudbury, but it is mostly English. A couple of years ago, Ontario francophones were awarded their first French community college after years of begging. Can Québec anglos complain about similar treatment?

In most cases language proficiency depends on parents and the importance they place on French. But adolescents have a way of rebelling against the older generation's wishes, and even strong parental commitment is often wasted as the young drift into the easiness and social acceptance of living in the language of the majority. In fact, it is not unusual to find that students from anglophone families become better in French than Franco-Ontarians because the best of them are there to learn the language for self-betterment and solid economic reasons.

I wasn't surprised to hear an educator speaking at an Ottawa seminar recount his experience, in 1992, on asking teenagers in a French high school what language they spoke in their day-to-day lives. He will always remember the girl who turned to her best friend in the class to say: "When we speak to each other, we speak French, don't we?" She asked the question in English.

Le Droit, the newspaper created to fight Regulation 17, exposed a situation in Kingston, in the winter of 1992, where the French school was located in a series of "portable" classrooms — trailers really. To add insult to injury, they were located in the school yard of the English high school. I don't know of too many cases like that for anglophones in Québec.

In Thunder Bay, local authorities still insisted in 1992 on not providing French public instruction for sixteen children whose parents demanded only a "multi-age" classroom since they didn't want them to attend under the Catholic system. The Ontario law states that instruction in French must be provided where only one child is involved, and, if necessary, arrangements can be made with neighbouring school boards to provide it. In Thunder Bay, they came up with the bright idea of bussing the sixteen students 180 miles away, to Nakina, and to pay their room and board for the week, something that couldn't have cost any less than giving them a small spot locally.

In Penetanguishene, fights erupted on Camp Borden, the Armed Forces base, when anglophone children were confronted with unilingual French kids from Québec whose parents were serving there. The teachers had to intervene to stop the fist fights as the Québec children wondered what hell they had just descended into.

My sister Ginette, an ex-school teacher who went on to hold a director's position with the Ontario French Teachers' Association and now does work within the Franco-Ontarian community across the province, made in 1991 roughly the same tour I did fifteen years earlier.

She remembers asking a French high school student in Welland's Confederation School where the library was. He didn't understand what a "bibliothèque" was.

But that's not the only drama. "French is a dead language in Ontario," she says. "It's not only that the young speak bad French; they are ashamed to speak it. Perhaps parents are becoming more conscious of the problem, but the kids speak more and more English at home."

And the enemy within the francophone population is a growing monster, since Franco-Ontarians are more and more sharply divided on whether their kids should attend public or separate schools. By being so, they inevitably dilute their own strength to the point where many school boards are on the verge of government receivership.

So, while Québécois are fighting anglophones and immigrants, Franco-Ontarians are struggling with their own progeny. It is a losing battle and only a matter of time. In New Brunswick, Québec's proximity; the strong concentration of francophones, Acadians, and Québec expatriates in the north of the province; and progressive government policies by premiers Richard Hatfield and Frank McKenna seem to have given new life to the will to survive and prosper. No francophones anywhere in the country have demonstrated this through their painful history more than the Acadians have. In the West, French-immersion schools produce bilingual Canadians as never before, but francophones who have survived as such in Manitoba, especially, and in Alberta, to a lesser degree, are the product of a small miracle. Despite widespread intolerance, St-Boniface College still churns out francophone graduates — although, to be truthful, English is the language of choice outside the classroom. It is the same in Edmonton, where the Oblates have carried the load for much of the twentieth century. But where are we headed, when a premier like Don Getty says in 1992 that bilingualism policies have to be abandoned? What's happening in New Brunswick when the anti-French CORE party wins eight seats and forms the official opposition? What if Québec splits?

In this respect, for all their determination, Franco-Ontarians, and other French minorities, who want the tradition — if nothing else — to survive have only Québec to count on. If it ever leaves Canada, it will bring an end to an agony that began a long time ago.

There will be those like myself who will go on functioning in English, while not being afraid to say they are francophone. But we will become tolerated objects of curiosity, anachronisms in a society where our children and their children will find nothing in common with their past in a present that leaves them little room for French.

The Franco-Ontarian anthem, recently written by singer-composer Paul Demers, is aptly titled "Notre place," our place "today for tomorrow." That is all Franco-Ontarians are looking for: a little bit of space to preserve what is left of what was once a nation.

But chances are the schools that, like Ecole Guigues, became monuments to the resistance, will remain just that: buildings with a past but little meaning in a world that has chosen to forget. And forgetting the past, as English Canada is discovering, can be dangerous: it can certainly be argued that they should have, but French Canadians have not forgotten.

POLITICS:
Rebels, Heroes, and Uncle Toms

‽ ‽ ‽

NOWHERE MORE THAN IN THE conduct of politics do Québécois live up to the sacred words engraved on their licence plates: "Je me souviens." They remember the Plains of Abraham — or at least their version of it and its importance — they remember Louis Riel, they remember conscription and the beaches of Dieppe, they remember Clyde Wells and the Meech Lake Accord failure. And, should they commit the ultimate sin and forget, as all people do between elections, they will always find the leaders to remind them of the "humiliations" they were subjected to during their history and their struggle for respect and survival within Canada.

This chapter deals mainly with Québec politics and the province's relationship with Ottawa — mostly since the Quiet Revolution — because they overshadow any political fights French Canadians elsewhere may have waged. Although it has conveniently abandoned the defence of francophones in other provinces, Québec remains the only strong political card in the French Canadians' hand. When it speaks, the English majority listens, if only because they fear that, otherwise, Québécois will do something drastic. In that sense, although some francophones outside Québec would argue that Québécois' constant bickering and demands have greatly hindered their relations with the English majority, they would still have to admit that, without Québec's threatening politics, policies like bilingualism and public French education would never have been implemented.

Québec's relations with Ottawa have historically been marked by distrust — often mutual. The feeling explains in part why Québécois have voted as a monolithic bloc time and again to preserve what was coined "French Power" at the federal level. If the re-election of a given party depended on their mood swings, Québécois felt they could get what they wanted no matter how unqualified or incompetent their elected MPS were. Brian Mulroney, for instance, swept into power with a slate of relatively unknown and untested candidates.

Since the Quiet Revolution, however, the people of Québec have gradually attached more importance to provincial politics and counted on successive premiers to show their might against the federal government. Thus they have switched parties and leaders in Québec City, depending on the times and on whether they thought they had to be aggressive to the point of blackmail (equality or independence) or more conciliatory, in tough economic downturns, for instance. They have been as ambivalent towards Canada in their politics as in their souls. They crave a form of sovereignty, but still can't quite bring themselves to just say goodbye to Canada, the country they helped build.

While they once considered every French Canadian to be one of theirs — a "Canadien" — they gradually retreated behind their borders to develop nationalism at home and came to see Québec as the only political entity that mattered in their quest for respect, survival, and prosperity. Through the Maurice Duplessis era, from 1944 to 1959, their brand of "nationalisme" was largely considered to be a parochial affair. Duplessis exploited it to form a coalition of "nationalistes," the church, and the farmers, which Québec's urban intelligentsia could not defeat. But the phenomenon was still a local one as the former Union Nationale premier turned on the rhetoric to win four elections in a row, virtually unchallenged.

The turbulent 1960s came, and Québec nationalism, with all its symbols and demands, spilled over the province's frontier to splash all of Canada. The English majority, confronted with a beast more ferocious than ever suspected, asked, justifiably: "What does Québec want?" To have its cake and eat it too, would have been an acceptable answer.

It would take some time for English Canada to understand how deeply rooted the "nationaliste" phenomenon had become in Québec and how it could only gain strength. An entire society had grown up behind its protective walls, had learned to read and write, but, most important, had learned to think for itself and put the rediscovered Québec nation first rather than compromise with the Canadian majority. It had happened discreetly, almost secretly. But, by 1960, Québécois were poised to strike and they would do so more dramatically than ever before, upsetting their own traditional values and preparing for an unprecedented showdown with the rest of Canada. The Parti Québécois would soon become the vehicle for their collective will.

On November 15, 1976, when I walked out of the Gatineau polling booth, I felt as if I had just cast a protest vote. I had been living on the Québec side of the river for two years, and the politics of the restless province had me hooked. Over the previous four years, I had grown increasingly uneasy with federalism, particularly the bleak future I saw for French minorities within the system. René Lévesque had charmed me, while a young Robert Bourassa was leading a government in which corruption and patronage seemed to be as widespread as it had been during the Duplessis regime. Not only did the Parti Québécois appear to offer the best alternative as a government, but its sovereignty-association option was, I thought, the best hope for the survival of the French-Canadian nation on North American soil. It was the only way to control our destiny. Besides, like those of many Québécois, my doubts about separation had been appeased by the PQ's promise to hold a referendum on the matter. Whereas in the two previous elections a vote for Lévesque had meant instant sovereignty, we now had the option to reconsider the matter later.

Still, no one could have guessed that a separatist vote in my riding would have much effect on the results. After all, not only was Jean Alfred a largely unproven candidate for the Parti Québécois, running in a riding bordering on Ottawa that was no fertile breeding-ground for the separatist option, but he was a black Haitian immigrant. Not a betting man's dream horse.

That unforgettable night, the Québécois left me — and the country — shell-shocked. Alfred was one of 69 Lévesque disciples who had just steamrolled over the province, where they had held only 7 of 110 seats three years earlier.

The Messiah of sovereignty, who had buried his separatist option into a platform promising "good government," had reduced Robert Bourassa's despised Liberals to only twenty-eight seats, with the briefly revitalized Union Nationale grabbing eleven, thanks largely to the support of disenchanted anglophones and federalists.

In Montréal's Centre Paul Sauvé, where, six years earlier, FLQ sympathizers had gathered before the imposition of the War Measures Act threw many of them in jail without just cause, the people's hero, "Ti-Poil" Lévesque — as they affectionately called him — was drowned out by the cheers of a euphoric crowd and the sound of the campaign song: "A partir d'aujourd'hui, demain nous appartient" ("Starting with today, tomorrow belongs to us").

I was too flabbergasted at the giant step Québec society had just taken into uncertainty to celebrate the small part I had played in it. Even Lévesque echoed the sentiments of a disbelieving people when he said from the podium that he had expected to win, but never so decidedly.

I remember my late father-in-law a few days before the vote, sitting at the end of the kitchen table with a worried look on his face. A Franco-Ontarian from the north of the province and a wise man, he asked me about the election and, without listening much to my answer, which was that a PQ victory was virtually impossible, said: "I don't know. . . . Québec — when they change sides, they change sides." And, as if he were holding the province's voters in his hands, he made a flipping motion. That image has always stayed with me, because, on that night, I thought he didn't know what he was talking about. What he was predicting seemed too far-fetched.

After all, many of those Québécois who so resoundingly brought Lévesque to power were the same ones who had elected Pierre Elliott Trudeau in 1968, saved him from defeat in 1972, and given him another majority in 1974. And, three years later, in 1979, they would deprive Joe Clark of a total victory; in February 1980 they would contribute seventy-four seats (out of seventy-five in Québec) to Trudeau's resurrection. Many of them would go on three months later to reject Lévesque's referendum before re-electing him against all odds the following year.

Why? Are they just bullheaded, or devilishly clever? Most befuddled observers have found two main reasons over the years for one of the most baffling two-timing love affairs Canada has ever known: how could the same passionate and politically charged people vote at the same time for Lévesque and Trudeau?

On paper, of course, it didn't make sense, given the two radically different visions of Canada offered by the two leaders.

There has always been the obvious explanation of the "tribal" vote. Being a minority in Canada, the theory goes, Québécois stick with their favourite son, whatever his policies may be. Once they have their man in Ottawa, they feel free to rock the boat at home and elect their true spiritual leaders, those who will defend them against the English tide.

That theory is, of course, simplistic.

The other theory — which goes hand in hand with the first — assumes a lot more shrewdness on the part of the deceptively fickle Québec electorate. They have been accused of "hedging their bets," getting the best of both worlds by making sure they vote as a bloc. Their federal vote is so crucial to the winner in Ottawa that re-election without them is improbable, even impossible.

John Diefenbaker tried it without their support in 1957, and fell short of a majority. In 1958, with Maurice Duplessis's backing and organization, he scored the greatest majority win up to that time, but he barely survived with a minority in 1962 when the Québécois deserted him by electing an incredible twenty-six Social Credit MPs and thirty-five Grits against only fourteen Tories. In 1958, with Duplessis's blessing on the podium and his election thugs helping "persuade" voters at the polling stations, Diefenbaker had captured an unprecedented fifty out of seventy-five ridings.

And so the Québécois have been callously characterized as simply "going with the winner." Even Tory blacksheep minister Marcel Masse infuriated his boss, Brian Mulroney, when, after the Tories' record 211-seat victory in 1984, he hinted at such a nasty streak in the province's voters.

Masse said privately that the Québécois had decided to vote Conservative only because they realized they might be left out in the cold if they didn't go with the man the rest of Canada had already chosen as its next prime minister. I was at Mulroney's side when he learned of the unreliable Masse's antics. He was beside himself, since he believed he had won Québec cleanly on a "national reconciliation" platform and a promise to repair the damage done by Trudeau.

The prime minister was at least partly right. Marcel Masse is a loner with a grand delusion à la Charles de Gaulle; he has seldom seen any merit in any politician other than Marcel Masse. To illustrate the point, when his followers celebrated Masse's twenty-five years in political life, in 1991, the minister had a video of his life and times made in which the narrator explained that, after being forced out of provincial politics, he remained "en réserve de la République" ("at the beck and call of the Republic"), as de Gaulle had done in his first retirement.

In any case, Mulroney may have had a point: the reality could just be that it is the aspiring winner who courts Québec, not the other way around. In fact, in 1988, when the polls put the Tories in trouble against John Turner's surging Liberals, Mulroney was personally convinced that he had to convert Québécois to his cause first, and that Ontarians would be the ones to fall in line and ensure the majority. He firmly believed enough of the voters in Québec would not risk seeing a government elected without their strong support. But who among the political pundits on both sides of the fence is right? Is it Québec or Ontario that likes to go with the winner?

It is also interesting to note that, had Mulroney not won a single seat in Québec in 1984, he could still technically have formed a majority government with 153 ridings. Chances are, however, if he hadn't convinced his own compatriots to abandon the Liberals in droves, the rest of the country would not have been so easily won over either. In fact, it was the rest of Canada that took a chance on Mulroney's promise of reconciliation, as the Tories themselves had heeded his warning a year earlier in the leadership race, when he claimed the party had lost more than 100 seats by steadfastly refusing to elect a grass-roots Québécois as leader. Again, in 1988, the Tory strategy was to secure Québec first; the rest of the country would follow.

But does any of this really explain the Trudeau–Lévesque phenomenon?

For all their emotionalism and apparent recklessness, Québécois are a very cautious and choosy bunch when it comes to electing their leaders.

"It will always remain a mystery to me," says Arthur Tremblay. "Why is it that when we [Québécois] are on the verge of making a breakthrough to affirm our identity, we always manage to position ourselves to make sure we lose?"

The magus from the Saguenay shakes his head when he thinks back to 1980, when Québécois massively rejected Joe Clark — who was open to their aspirations for meaningful constitutional reform — to re-elect Trudeau, who was a sworn enemy of anything but a strong central government. Tremblay worked for the "Non" side in the referendum, but he admits that he started doubting his commitment when Trudeau spoke in Montréal during the campaign. "I went back home and I told my wife that, for all his previous promises of renewal, he hadn't promised anything at all! But it was too late by then to change my mind."

At the same time, as a columnist for *Le Droit*, I was writing that Trudeau was asking for "a blank cheque" from the Québécois. There was nothing new in what he had to say while praising the beauties and merits of Canada from coast to coast in a speech reminiscent of the 1972 "The Land Is Strong" campaign.

Senator Tremblay was just as baffled, in spring 1992, by Premier Robert Bourassa's latest manoeuvring, promising a provincial referendum on the upcoming federal constitutional offers rather than on sovereignty, and thereby reducing his leverage for real change by minimizing the threat of a vote on separation.

It is an enigma, and I can think of only one logical reason for it: fear. It may be true, as many have said, that Québécois hedge their bets in elections and major collective decisions like the referendum. But I suspect that it is not the rest of Canada they seek protection from. They are afraid of themselves.

Things have simply been going too far, too fast, and, once in a while, I think Québécois try to slow down the locomotive that went out of control three decades ago. In the end, as they are a very individualistic people in their social behaviour, it only makes sense that they be conservative in their political attitudes. And for all the loud noises and separatist threats they have made over the years, Québécois remain fundamentally conservative, concerned with comfort and money. If you scratch the surface a little, you will find out that most of them just want to be left alone to go on with their lives. The "revolution" wasn't "quiet" by accident. Anything more drastic would have alienated the people, as happened when they voted the Union Nationale back in with Daniel Johnson to slow the education reforms.

There is almost a pattern to it, at least since the days of Duplessis.

In 1960, Québécois shook off sixteen years of Union Nationale rule and embraced Jean Lesage's slogan that it was time for change. When his reforms started to frighten them, with their weakening church masters still holding some power over them, they sought comfort in Daniel Johnson and the more conservative Union Nationale they had found shameful only six years before.

When successive Union Nationale leaders Johnson and Bertrand tangled with their new-found Ottawa heroes — Trudeau, Jean Marchand, and Gérard Pelletier — on the question of Québec sovereignty, and the separatists became confused in the public's mind with the terrorist FLQ, they found refuge in a young Bourassa, the Liberal party, and a promise of 100,000 jobs thanks to Hydro-Québec's James Bay project.

In 1970, when Trudeau imposed the War Measures Act and sent the army into Québec, the majority didn't seem to flinch much as, in the middle of the crisis, they gave Montréal mayor Jean Drapeau, an Ottawa sympathizer, his greatest majority ever. Speaking of Drapeau, his twenty-six-year reign as mayor of Montréal, through the stormy times from 1960 to 1986, may be the surest indication of Québécois' profound desire for stability in the face of change.

After Bourassa's shaky six years at the helm of the province, as Québec was on the verge of social disorder with the trade unions at their most militant and backed by the Parti Québécois for its own political reasons, they elected the PQ, which had won no more than seven seats in two elections and had seen its charismatic leader, Lévesque, defeated twice in his own riding.

Then came Trudeau's unexpected return and a referendum slap in the face to Lévesque, followed by a friendly pat on the back to make up in 1981. The PQ won almost 50 per cent of the popular vote, nine more percentage points than in 1976, although during those four years, Claude Ryan's Liberals were elected in seventeen by-elections in a row. The self-righteous former *Le Devoir* editor-in-chief had been claiming for two years that the Lévesque government was "illegitimate."

Why did Québécois ultimately reject Ryan? They were afraid of a man who said "the hand of God" had led him into politics. They would rather stick with Lévesque, who was closer to the sinners they all were.

During his second mandate, Lévesque appeared more and more disillusioned and demoralized as Pierre Trudeau, having finally patriated the constitution from Britain without the support of the PQ government, prepared for his final exit. Enter Brian Mulroney, a man without a real party in Québec, who had to count on a bizarre coalition of nationalists eager to settle the score with the Ottawa Grits and disaffected provincial Liberals feeling betrayed by Trudeau's empty promises. Lévesque praised his triumph and his call for reconciliation by saying it was "un beau risque" ("an attractive risk"). Ti-Poil's days in politics and among the living were, however, already numbered. A tired man, he passed the torch to Pierre-Marc Johnson, son of former premier Daniel, who himself tried to steer the separatist party towards a surprisingly moderate position that virtually eliminated Article 1 of the constitution of the PQ, which set Québec independence as its first and main goal.

That would not prevent one of the most incredible political comebacks of our time, as the once maligned but now more mature Robert Bourassa recaptured the Liberal magic and power in the province. Québécois didn't hand it back to him, though, without a stern warning about the use they could make of their voting power, as Bourassa lost by more than two hundred votes to the PQ candidate in the riding of Bertrand. The province snickered collectively at this latest uniquely Québécois trick, while the new premier without a seat was reminded brutally of the changing moods of his people. Mulroney, for his part, rejoiced in having a personal friend running the province and jumped at the opportunity to strike the unfinished constitutional deal with Québec. Meech Lake happened in a public-opinion vacuum; Canadians and Québécois, by and large, had other things on their minds. Re-enter the spoiler, Pierre Trudeau and his cohorts, Jean Chrétien, Frank McKenna,

Clyde Wells, and Sharon Carstairs. Bourassa, facing re-election, panicked and, despite a ruling of the Supreme Court to the contrary, invoked the notwithstanding clause and passed Bill 178 maintaining the ban of English on commercial signs in Québec. English Canada roared at the "distinct society." By June 1990, a re-elected Mulroney had been devastated by the rejection of the Meech Lake Accord and had suffered a crushing personal blow in the loss of his long-time friend Lucien Bouchard, who quit the cabinet to lead the separatist Bloc Québécois. On June 25, it seemed that all of Montréal had taken to the streets with fleur-de-lys flags as Québécois appeared angrier and more determined than ever to go their own way. Bourassa bid for time by creating the Bélanger-Campeau commission on the future of Québec, a rigged affair that could only result in demands exceeding the terms of Meech Lake. Predictably it did, forcing the government to hold a referendum on sovereignty by the fall of 1992.

As of spring 1992, the polls steadily show the pro-separation option is losing ground with the Québécois, who would have favoured it by 65 per cent in the torrid summer following the failure of Meech. As we have seen, Bourassa has now said that he intends to hold the referendum on the federal government's offers, not sovereignty, thus delaying the possibility of separation, at least for the time being.

La Presse editorialist Alain Dubuc writes that, in fact, he is only the mirror of the ambivalence of his own people.

If this whirlwind, simplified history of the last thirty years leaves your head spinning, you probably feel like most Québécois. Their crazy "danse-hésitation" of one step forward, two steps back — or vice versa — is the surest sign that the Quiet Revolution is far from over, and that the people of Québec themselves have a hard time coming to terms with all its implications. The Québécois make a bold move one day and retreat behind the barricades the next. At times, it's a lot like Michael Jackson's "moonwalk," seeming to move forward when you're actually backing up.

Afraid of themselves. Conscious of their power, but terrified at the prospect they might abuse it. The uncertainty and the confusion inevitably lead to the classic bottom line: How much will independence cost? The dream is beautiful, but is it possible? A majority of Québécois, in a crunch, will fall back on the teachings of the clergy in their *collèges classiques*, who reminded us constantly of the old proverb: "Un tiens vaut mieux que deux tu l'auras" ("A bird in the hand is worth two in the bush").

The National Film Board produced a film called *Le confort et l'indifférence*, about the referendum campaign, whose thesis was that, in the end, 60 per cent of Québécois — including a clear majority of francophones — voted "Non" for fear of losing their standard of living or simply because they didn't care enough about their true identity. It is a valid theory only if you accept that your financial future and security should not outweigh an intangible vision of greatness associated with political sovereignty. But it is fundamentally unfair to condemn those who dare to focus on such down-to-earth considerations, and to brand them as traitors to the race. Yet, through the four years leading up to the crucial plebiscite, the Lévesque government had taken care to paint everything to do with a sovereign Québec in rosy hues. If you weren't with them, you were against them; unfaithful to the new religion, you were destined to be destroyed by the inner hell in your tortured and guilt-ridden soul, as you preferred the passing pleasures of a worthless life to the sacrifices that would bring you paradise.

Only against this complex background can the Trudeau-Lévesque puzzle be explained in part, if never completely.

The Québécois needed René Lévesque because he gave them pride in themselves. He pushed forward, as a possessed coach does his team, "a people," as he said in 1977, "that until now had been content to be forgotten, in order to survive."

They wanted Pierre Trudeau because they needed another superior intellect to remind them that even a revolution could not free them of their greater responsibilities to themselves and their duty to history — past, present, and future. Their ancestors had discovered and colonized all of Canada, francophone minorities still existed elsewhere, and they needed the political clout of Québec within the federation to survive in the future.

The first time I met René Lévesque was as unexpected as it was innocuous. I was just starting out in journalism and had been assigned to what was then the garbage heap of the sports department. That meant working nights and hours that severely limited my social life. On slow nights, our main objective on the sports desk was to wrap up the paper quickly so we could beat the 3:00 a.m. last call in Hull.

And so, there I was, closer to 4:00 a.m., going through my usual routine of walking over to the Hôtel Duvernay's front desk to have them call me a cab.

All of a sudden, a short figure appeared beside me at

the desk and told the attendant: "Tomorrow morning, at ten, in my room, a Scotch . . . double." I turned to face "Ti-Poil" himself, who was then campaigning in the 1973 election. Like a kid who had just bumped into a rock star, I introduced myself enthusiastically. He seemed more annoyed than charmed.

What struck me then was how short he was and how deceptively ordinary he looked. Somehow, I was just as surprised by that quality two years later, when he came out of his Montréal office, in PQ headquarters, to unceremoniously motion me to follow him for an extensive interview.

But behind the little chain-smoking man in the suit that seemed too big for him, I quickly discovered an intensely brilliant individual with a defiance in his eyes that warned you he was not one to be messed with. There seemed to be no end to his answers; interminable sentences came tumbling out like an avalanche.

When I mentioned Trudeau, he barely flinched, but made a point of saying the man had never been his friend — although many pundits at the time used to refer to earlier days when they had apparently been close. He said: "Jean Marchand was my friend. . . . He still is. I saw him on a plane the other day. But Trudeau had this disdainful face, this mommy's boy side."

Gérard Pelletier would later recount how he introduced Lévesque to Trudeau in the cafeteria of Radio-Canada in Montréal. René was already a television star then, and Trudeau was just a little-known troubleshooter who had shunned his rich background to support leftist causes, mainly through his stinging writings in the small but influential magazine *Cité Libre*.

After they were introduced, Trudeau suavely congratulated Lévesque on his show, before asking him scornfully: "But do you know how to write?" He wanted him to collaborate with him at *Cité Libre*. Lévesque tried to explain he had little time for free-lancing, and Trudeau, typically, became more contemptuous. As Pelletier tells it, René finally got up from his chair and shot back, laughing: "You're just a damn intellectual!"

"Their relationship remained pretty much the same after that," says Pelletier.

As for Trudeau, like many members of the press, I had a few skirmishes with him over the years, but he wasn't as approachable as Lévesque. I knew Trudeau only as most people did, from a distance. Jean Marchand once said of the man I had believed was his close friend: "He doesn't have any friends. . . . He gets along great with women, though."

Jean Chrétien had his own story to illustrate Trudeau's peculiar human warmth. On a government flight back from the Maritimes once, he sat down beside the prime minister and tried to make conversation by saying: "It's raining outside."

Trudeau replied: "When it rains, it's always outside." They didn't exchange another word for the remainder of the trip.

It didn't help that he also had the reputation, with those who knew him well, of being a penny pincher. Marchand would laugh at that while discussing it. Former famous French parliamentary correspondent Jean-Marc Poliquin, who died in 1983, liked to tell the story of how he was once invited to 24 Sussex with a small group of political thinkers and doers. "At some point, Trudeau said he was going to bed. But before going upstairs, he made sure he locked the liquor cabinet," Poliquin said, laughing.

In that sense, he was radically different from René

Lévesque, a typical Québécois "bon vivant," who also liked women, a little Scotch, and all-night poker games, often with journalists. And these different aspects of their personalities filtered down to the people who naturally identified more with "Ti-Poil" than with condescending Trudeau.

It has often been said that Lévesque was more emotional — therefore more Latin and "Québécois" — than cool-as-a-cucumber Pierre. I rather think that Trudeau had his emotions more under control, but was so tightly wrapped he could just as well explode when you least expected it. Like the day he almost came to blows in the lobby of the Commons with Québec union leader Michel Chartrand, whom he knew well. Or the "fuddle-duddle" incident. To be fair, in both cases he was seriously provoked.

Lévesque, on the other hand, sometimes appeared to be in a state of perpetual eruption.

But, despite appearances, the two men were very much alike. Both passionate, they had different and exciting lives before jumping into politics; Trudeau as a globetrotter to the most troubled and exotic places in the world, Lévesque as a war correspondent with the American army during the Second World War and with Radio-Canada in Korea. Both were educated at prestigious institutions that were then reputed to form the leaders of the future, Trudeau at Montréal's Jesuit Collège Brébeuf and Lévesque at Québec's Jesuit Collège Charles Garnier. Both were at the top of their class, although Trudeau seemed to enjoy studying law, while fun-loving Lévesque spent most of his university days playing cards from morning to night. They both dodged the draft in their own way, Lévesque taking the unusual step of joining the American army at twenty-one, rather than be conscripted into the Canadian forces when it became evident his absenteeism would prevent him from graduating third-year law. Trudeau, three years his senior, found other methods of staying away from the front, something that would dog him later in his political life, as journalists, mainly from the English media, would question his wartime record, or lack of it. He would eventually become a professor of law at the University of Montréal; René would pursue a career in radio and television.

Most importantly, neither of them ever expected to end up as leader of a people looking for answers, and both were dragged into politics more by events than by personal desire.

The two men have retained, one in death and the other in retirement, a fiercely loyal constituency in Québec. Nationalists speak, eyes brimming, of "Our Father René," while federalist Grits long for the glory days when the great Pierre used to tell them what to say and do. His partisans, especially women, love the septuagenarian Trudeau as much as his enemies despise him.

But whether they loved or hated the two French-Canadian leaders, most people feared them. And there is perhaps the greatest similarity between these men whose ideas were so diametrically opposed they became confused with the visceral hatred they had for each other.

René Lévesque and Pierre Trudeau were simply not individuals capable of being governed by those they considered to be lesser than themselves. Chances are, had Trudeau not won the Liberal leadership in 1968, he would have been bored with federal politics long before 1984. Lévesque eventually chose to resign — after threatening to do so often in times of trouble — rather than be ousted by his own party.

They, unlike many current politicians, agreed with Machiavelli that it is far better for the Prince to be feared than to be loved. And, in that sense, they were both bullies, with a deadly wit, capable of publicly humiliating their enemies, no matter how weak or puny. They wouldn't appreciate the comparison, but this approach to politics was also Maurice Duplessis's.

To their admirers — and they were legion — they were strong men, single-minded and driven, both conquerors of women. They'd pick a fight with anybody, anywhere, just to prove they weren't afraid to do so. Trudeau impressed with his athletic skills and his love of sports cars and motorcycles; Lévesque was the tough little punk with the cigarette dangling from the corner of his mouth.

In these respects they were both "macho," and Québécois like macho politicians. They still long for them, as the Americans still await the appearance of a John Kennedy.

That being said, should Trudeau attempt another comeback today — something misguided Grits still dream of — he might have a rougher time in Québec than he used to. When he showed up for René Lévesque's funeral in Montréal, in November 1987, he was heckled and booed by the crowd. His Meech Lake stance was immensely unpopular with separatists and federalists alike, and Jean Chrétien, for one, cannot shake his gigantic shadow.

Trudeau and Lévesque are both yesterday's men. But what a day it was! And if you go back farther, to Duplessis, you'll find in Québécois a natural inclination to support no-nonsense authoritarian leaders. Among themselves, the men — there were few women — at the top of the pyramid have often found it difficult to work with, let alone stand each other. They have even shown a propensity to insult each other publicly.

Trudeau called Robert Bourassa a "hot-dog eater," and Jean Drapeau referred to him once as "Le Petit Robert." That was a play on the title on the famous French dictionary: the Montréal mayor said he had "consulted Le Petit Robert." But it was also an allusion to Bourassa's small stature in the Québécois eyes. He was not a man to be feared.

René Lévesque and Pierre Bourgault, one of the pioneers of the separatist movement, couldn't stand each other. There was no love lost between Jean Chrétien and Claude Ryan, although they worked actively together on the "Non" committee for several weeks during the 1980 referendum campaign. Now, while there have been no public clashes between them, backroom manoeuvring has heightened the tension between Jacques Parizeau, current leader of the PQ, and the Bloc Québécois's Lucien Bouchard, the one many would like to see take Parizeau's place.

These relatively open personal conflicts have not only made the Québec political scene colourful, but left the impression it is always on the verge of blowing up.

In one of life's great paradoxes — but typically Québécois — Lévesque would be largely responsible for creating the politicians who would later defy and defeat his dream as the three "Wise Men" — known in French as the "trois colombes" ("three doves") — Trudeau, Marchand, and Pelletier, would join the federal Liberal party.

Their main reason for jumping into politics was that they were convinced Confederation was in trouble. Strong French Canadians were needed in Ottawa, and in the mid-1960s their representation was dismal. The other reason, Lévesque told me in an interview, was that Trudeau, especially, had developed a low opinion of the Québec government over the years and didn't want to waste himself in such a small-minded nationalist environment. It didn't matter to him what Lévesque was trying to do; he still perceived Québec nationalism through the narrow prism of the despotic Duplessis era.

These were men who, like the rest of Québécois, had seen a government controlling every aspect of their daily lives, from the police to the church, to the universities, the media, and, of course, government contracts. They saw little hope for change from the inside.

Lévesque, for his part, after leading the fight to nationalize hydro-electricity, had made up his mind by 1963 that Québec sovereignty was the most viable option — but he waited until a Liberal electoral defeat to make his move in 1967.

Even then, he first tried to have his sovereignty-association platform adopted by the provincial Liberal party, but was soundly defeated at the convention. It does give an indication, though, that in spite of his image as a dangerous radical, Lévesque was very much a moderate.

Later, he would also shun Pierre Bourgault's approaches for a merger because he didn't like the image of the Ralliement pour l'Indépendance Nationale. "To him, we were the bums of the independence movement," Bourgault would later say. "We were always in jail or in the streets, protesting." And that created confusion in the people's minds with the terrorist FLQ whose plantings of bombs were not seen as heroic acts by the tranquil Québec population who, despite its revolution, had been used to law and order.

In one of his first speeches as leader of the Parti Québécois, Lévesque denounced corruption in the old parties, both the Union Nationale and the Liberals, who
had been bribed into subjugating Québécois by the
"WASP" establishment of the province, which was widely
believed to be a major contributor to election slush-
funds. In one fell swoop, he had touched the two sensitive chords that had bothered Québécois about their
governments and the ways of their society for many
years. The first one was the selling-out of their politicians to the people with money; the other was the domination they had suffered themselves under those with
money who spoke English.

Once elected, he perhaps didn't realize that, with Bill
101 and the new measures he put in place to practically
eliminate patronage and institute "popular financing"
of political parties in Québec — still the only province
to operate without corporate donations — he had already taken care of the two main problems that bothered his people.

In Ottawa, he had involuntarily contributed to put in
place the forces that would stop his drive for independence, and in Québec, he had eliminated many of the
obvious reasons for it. When they were faced with the
decision, in 1980, a majority of Québécois believed that,
for the moment, the revolution had gone far enough.
And there were French Canadians they respected in Ottawa to tell them that.

But where does that leave us today?

First, with a Québec society in which "nationalism"
is no longer a dirty word, whatever Pierre Trudeau says.
It is no longer identified with the Union Nationale's des-
pot and, in fact, Duplessis was made into a sort of hero
by the PQ themselves when his towering bronze statue

was given a prominent spot near the Assemblée nationale. In the late 1970s, Radio-Canada also aired a tremendously popular TV series on Duplessis in which the man's love of his province again turned him into a hero, despite all his sins against his people.

The PQ nationalists cleaned up the political environment and greatly affected the politics of other parties: witness the provincial Liberal party itself, whose "youth wing" sometimes gives the impression of going farther towards sovereignty than Lévesque ever did. There is no turning back for Québécois nationalism now. The only question that remains to be answered is whether the idea of a "nation" — a people rather than a state — can co-exist with the idea of Canada as we now know it. I very much doubt it can.

This is one reality both Brian Mulroney and Robert Bourassa have understood; Jean Chrétien is still struggling to come to grips with it and his own outdated federalist beliefs.

Where Mulroney fits in Québec politics is like many of the things about him — not obvious or easy to grasp.

Many Canadians have asked me over the years: "What is he really? English or French?" Of course, he's of Irish descent. If we didn't know by his name, his temper would give it away.

There's no doubt Mulroney is more comfortable in the English language, especially writing it. His French is frankly almost as good, and if I didn't personally know he has occasional doubts about the proper use of certain words and expressions, there's no way a typical conversation would give his lack of assurance away.

In the early days he did have a funny habit, which amused the press gallery, of eliminating accents on some e's and adding them where they didn't belong, but his recent speeches indicate that he seems to have mastered that minor problem. In any case, when it was pointed out to him, he used to say simply that that was the way they spoke in Baie Comeau.

So you really can't judge whether he's anglophone or francophone merely by the way he speaks. In fact, his conversational French is superior to most Québécois'.

But he instinctively speaks the language he thinks the other person is most comfortable in. When I did my first interview with him, after quitting my job as his press secretary and becoming a columnist for *The Sun* two years later, he asked me, with a perplexed look: "We've always spoken French to each other, haven't we?" That was absolutely true. Our few English conversations took place when there were more than just the two of us. Even during the interview, which was conducted in English, he tended to switch to French when he really wanted to make a point. I know the feeling — Franco-Ontarians do this a lot too.

If you were to ask Mulroney what he is, he would no doubt tell you proudly that he's a Canadian. Politically, of course, he is.

But, in his heart and soul, Brian Mulroney is as Québécois as they come. His reflexes are those of a French Québécois. How could it be otherwise? He was brought up playing with unilingual French kids on the street. And if he did later attend an English university in the Maritimes, his most fruitful years were spent at Laval University, where he totally immersed himself in French-Canadian culture with friends such as Bernard Roy and Lucien Bouchard.

His political mentors were Daniel Johnson and Robert Cliche, two nationalists.

He refers to himself as a boy from Baie Comeau, but he really is a Montréalais. He adopted Montréal as his own and functioned well in both cultures in a city where they have traditionally been divided. But while the francophones naturally warmed up to him, he has never been totally accepted by certain snobbish elements of the anglophone community who perceive him as being too closely allied with the French. They still don't vote for him.

Brian Mulroney is not a Québec nationalist, but he could fake it any day — sometimes he does. He has always shied away, for instance, from debating the merits of Bill 101, or even Bill 178. He did so even after the folly of Bourassa's sign law became evident to him after the Supreme Court ruled that although French could have greater prominence on signs in Québec, other languages must be tolerated, if only in smaller print. (Polls show the people of Québec wouldn't mind this much today.)

Mulroney knows that it would be politically suicidal for him to join such debates because he has built his support on the fact that he could find a place in Canada for the province's nationalists. And that's why the failure of Meech Lake crushed him so.

It boxed him into a situation where he inevitably had to adopt a more traditionally federalist rhetoric, something he carefully avoided in his first six years in power.

At the same time, he has never really shared his knowledge and understanding of Québec nationalism with the rest of Canadians, because he doesn't think they would understand. This explains the vagueness of the "distinct society" clause and his reluctance to define it.

It is hard to put a finger on what French Québécois

think of Mulroney, though. It was certainly not love at first sight. Before he started messing up in the 1984 campaign, with the Iona Campagnolo "bum-patting" incident, dismal organization resulting from lack of preparedness and money, and a terrible performance in the televised debates, John Turner was ahead in the polls in Québec. Mulroney himself was even ten points behind the Liberal incumbent in his riding of Manicouagan. And, in 1988, the province's voters finally reluctantly toppled his way when all their political and business leaders told them free trade was the way of the future.

The Tory label didn't help, of course, in the province that had gradually erased every Conservative but local Joliette hero Roch LaSalle from its electoral map. But Mulroney himself, with his conciliatory attitudes and carefully chosen words, was not the kind of politician they were used to. How could they trust a man who refused to insult anybody? He was just too smooth to be true. He did have his moments, though, when he took a run at Liberal fixer and minister André Ouellet, the symbol of Ottawa Liberals' patronage and heavy hitting in the province. The Québécois liked it when he said they didn't have to be "the hostages of André Ouellet anymore." That was more like it.

Robert Bourassa has very much the same problem — but more acute, because it is coupled with an even stronger public perception of deviousness. His first stint in power between 1970 and 1976 did a lot to create that image among both French and English Québécois. Francophones blamed him for everything bad that happened in the province, including a scandal involving the sale of meat from diseased animals, a scandal he had nothing to do with; anglophones felt he had let them down with his language bill, Bill 22.

When he left for Europe after his 1976 defeat, he was, in everybody's mind, finished as a politician. "Bon débarras," or "good riddance," said Québécois. As it turns out, his temporary disappearance was the best thing that ever happened to him. He didn't come back in triumph either. He started giving speeches on the rubber-chicken circuit and, once Claude Ryan met with disaster and Raymond Garneau destroyed his chances by going to Ottawa with John Turner, it was the Liberal membership itself that begged him to return.

Bourassa still had a lot of friends within the party, but that was not obvious to the population at large. Still, he managed to come across as a model of stability for Québécois who had just emerged from the PQ years and the national recession. He could give them time to think and he did have one redeeming quality: he was a capable accountant.

Accountants are not known to be unusually exciting. But at that juncture, lack of excitement was what Québec wanted. A good administrator who would stay out of trouble and stay out of their way. Because, as *L'Actualité*'s January 1992 poll clearly showed, the average Québécois does not like government interference in his affairs, and the Parti Québécois had done a little too much of that. One of the greatest controversies concerned the introduction of state-controlled auto insurance, widely seen as a "socialist" measure.

Québec was very much tempted by "the left" in the 1970s, after the demise of traditional values and the Catholic church. Unions had attained unprecedented power and influence. Teachers, for instance, had pushed militancy to the point of saying that insisting on their students speaking correct French was a "bourgeois" attitude. Marxism was being discussed openly as a solution for the Québec worker.

But it never caught on. The biggest Québec union, the Fédération des travailleurs du Québec, headed by the legendary Louis Laberge, represented most construction workers, but it was about as leftist as its investment fund — a successful capitalist venture if ever there was one.

The Parti Québécois was seen as a social-democrat party, but that quickly changed after early measures, such as state-run auto insurance, were in place and the true free-enterprise nature of Lévesque, Parizeau, and Pierre-Marc Johnson came through.

Québécois have been left virtually with a void in terms of a socialist option, since the provincial New Democratic Party — as is its federal counterpart — is as marginal as it is bizarre in considering running former Pierre Laporte assassin Paul Rose as one of its candidates. But this absence of socialism so far doesn't seem to bother Québécois much.

Should the need be felt, the PQ or the Liberal party will easily adapt to it anyway. That's the way it's always been. As long as the "Canada question" isn't resolved, the voters have little time or energy for any other drastic changes.

Robert Bourassa certainly deserves his reputation for being chameleon-like. In fact, some see him more as a snake; in the mid-1970s wax statues of the premier in the shape of a cobra sold like hotcakes in Montréal.

I know him, though, as a very courteous, reasonable man. And his worst detractors do acknowledge, once they meet him, that he does have a unique kind of charm.

He has also matured greatly as a politician since his run-ins with Trudeau, who's not around to kick him anymore.

Bourassa is a consummate moderate, not given to extreme ideas or rhetoric. Like Mulroney, he is not a leader in the Quiet Revolution mould, and thus, although he can win elections, he fails to inspire his people.

But who says they can't sometimes vote with their minds rather than their hearts? As long as Mulroney and Bourassa hit the right buttons, convincing them that they can live and prosper within Canada, Québécois will listen to what they have to say — on the condition that it's what they want to hear. Passion will not be involved in their choice, as was the case with Lévesque and Trudeau, who brought out the best and the worst in themselves and their people.

Jean Chrétien only wishes he didn't have to deal with such passions. The "little guy from Shawinigan" had always been aware that a certain element of Québec's intelligentsia looked down on him as an inferior specimen of the race.

The roots of the problem lay in Chrétien's personality itself. With the deliberately exaggerated *joual* that seemed to serve him so well among the hard-working people of St-Maurice riding, Chrétien was exposing not only to them, but to the whole country, what the Québécois hated most in themselves.

He didn't seem to have the genius of Duplessis, who could be all things to all people, speaking *joual* to the uneducated of the rural areas, and then going head to head with the intellectuals of the clergy and the universities.

Chrétien's "ordinary guy" persona was too overwhelming, too — well, ordinary, and Québec's elite was horrified when he exported it to English Canada, giving speeches about being a frog and proud of it. Many of my Québec friends, whom I don't consider to be of the snobbish elite but certainly educated, thoughtful members of society, deserted the fiery federalist at that point.

Chrétien might have gotten away with his little-guy image, but what could not be forgiven was his federalist stance during Meech Lake. On the day almost every Québécois was cursing Newfoundland's Clyde Wells's name, he embraced him before the cameras for all to see, and thanked him for his fine work.

It was simply too much, even for the people of St-Maurice. Chrétien was shattered that summer, when he went to a local shopping centre on a simple errand and the people who a few years before would have welcomed him with open arms, insulted him, called him a traitor, and refused to shake his hand. He told friends privately about the one individual who did shake hands with him, then wiped his own on his pant leg. The extent of the damage he had done to himself in Québec then hit him.

Is it recoupable? The sentiment is certainly deep-rooted and not just a figment of the intelligentsia's imagination anymore. The "Uncle Tom" label has finally stuck to Chrétien in his own province, and it will be hard to shake.

Since Mulroney has been pushed by the mere existence of the Bloc Québécois to defend stronger federalism, he may himself have squeezed Chrétien out of the picture. Between two federalists, many Québécois will undoubtedly opt for the one who tried to accommodate their hopes, and shy away from the man who put his arms around Clyde Wells.

The fact is that there are very few true-blue francophone federalists left in the province. There are still many who accept the Canadian federation as the best option, but after the Quiet Revolution, after Trudeau, after Meech Lake, the public no longer feels any loyalty to Canada for the sake of Canada.

When the National Arts Centre symphony orchestra travels to Québec to celebrate the 125th anniversary of the country and is ordered not to play the national anthem, and the incident hardly causes a ripple in the province — although it provokes indignation elsewhere — it's clear how far things have gone.

In that sense, Québécois have once again parted company with their other French-Canadian cousins, especially Franco-Ontarians. They still see the federal government as the only government worth voting for, and Queen's Park as largely irrelevant. They also are still very much committed to the Liberal party and, by and large, didn't like Mulroney long before a majority of Canadians made up their minds about him.

For instance, in my riding of Ottawa-Vanier, perhaps the most Franco-Ontarian of all, in 1984, Liberal incumbent Jean-Robert Gauthier still got an 11,000-vote plurality. That was down from his usual majority of 20,000, but still, when most of the francophones in Québec and in New Brunswick sided with the Tories, Franco-Ontarians were the most reluctant to do so.

Mulroney did make a few inroads in ridings with a significant French population, but lost most of those seats in 1988, as French Canadians went back to their old habits of blindly voting Liberal. Whether it be in Manitoba or Ontario, they feel that, whenever they were persecuted, the Tories were involved. In New Brunswick, it took Richard Hatfield to change that trend. When he self-destructed, they went back to the Grits in droves.

The Liberals in Ottawa pushed for the Official Languages Act, which would provide protection for francophones across the country, while Mulroney — in spite of his brave stand in 1983, against his own party, in favour of language rights for Franco-Manitobans — was more preoccupied with satisfying Québec. A series of ugly anti-francophone incidents, including stamping on fleur-de-lys flags and refusing to provide services in French, swept English Canada, partly because of Mulroney's perceived surrender to Québec's demands.

In this respect, French-Canadian minorities are as much at the mercy of Québec's nationalists as is the English minority within its boundaries. The prospect of separation would mean the end of a dream for most of them, as, without the clout of six million francophone Québécois, they would become a forgotten people in their own country.

CULTURE:
Anything but "Alouette"

᷿   ᷿   ᷿

CULTURE — FRENCH CANADIANS, especially Québécois, have waged countless battles in the name of its
preservation and ultimate triumph. But like the knights
of the great Crusades, if our blind beliefs have always
held firm and carried us through the bloody battles, the
reason for our quest has been as elusive as the Holy
Grail. What is it we are fighting to preserve?

Ourselves, would be the obvious answer. But who are
we? What makes this culture so vital and its disappearance so life-threatening to us?

The answer may be found in the simple things.

First, as many English Canadians seem to believe,
French Canadians love to sing. But you should know
that we hate "Alouette." Anglophones could do a lot for
English-French relations by promising never to ask us
to sing it again. We'll still go for "Chevaliers de la table
ronde" on a bad night, but not "Alouette."

Robert Charlebois popularized a song with a chorus
that goes, in English: "I'm a frog, you're a frog, kiss me
and I'll turn into a prince suddenly. . . ." Then in French:
"Give me some peanuts and I'll sing you 'Alouette' on

key." It is, of course, a parody, but also a reflection of the fact that we see "Alouette" — and any requests to hear it — as the ultimate symbol of English condescension.

Many minorities or isolated groups, it seems, have found solace in music — I think of blacks in the United States and Maritimers in English Canada. We French Canadians do seem to launch into song at family or social gatherings more easily than English Canadians.

When I was a child, not a single family occasion went by without my father eventually bringing out his Hawaiian guitar — an oddity in those days — while an uncle in the room would follow the beat with a couple of spoons.

It was a rare Christmas or New Year's party during which no one asked my grandfather to get up and "jigue." It was as much a tradition as asking for his blessing. And funnier.

I was to discover later that we in Vanier were not alone in this respect. Quite the contrary, the songs we knew — whether they were traditional folk songs, called "chansons à répondre" because the group kept repeating the verses; religious hymns; or hits of the moment — were a common bond throughout French-Canadian society. You were expected to know these tunes and you were expected to have fun singing them.

Which explains, perhaps, why Gilles Vigneault's beautiful "Gens du pays" quickly became Québécois' national anthem, Like many of the great poet's songs, not only was it nationalist but it sounded like the folk music we had always sung. Like a "berceuse" ("lullaby"), it sang itself, and everybody could get in on the act.

So much so, in fact, that French Canadians eventually

desecrated it by using it to replace "Happy Birthday" or to congratulate a friend on a job promotion. As a result, it has lost much of its original meaning and impact. The song is, for instance, altered like this: instead of singing "Gens du pays, c'est à votre tour de vous laisser parler d'amour" (Roughly translated, in unpoetic terms: "People of the nation, your turn has come to hear words of love"), a group will sing, "Mon cher Michel, c'est à ton tour. . . ." Pretty harmless, corny stuff.

But anglophones who know what the song originally meant are often unaware that it has evolved into something else. A friend told me the story of how he went to an Ottawa restaurant in spring 1992, just when the constitutional debate was heating up. There was a group of francophone women there, obviously having a good time after work. At some point, they burst out into "Gens du pays," though they were really singing it to a friend on her birthday.

An insulted anglophone patron decided to retaliate by singing "O Canada." The women, needless to say, looked puzzled.

I understood at a very young age that to be able to sing and entertain was a status symbol in French-Canadian society. And I wanted desperately to do it. I used to spend hours on end in the basement, singing to records, many in English and with words I could pronounce but didn't understand. My brothers and I wanted to have a band like "Les Baronnets," a Québec trio who had enjoyed some success by translating mostly Beatles songs into French. "It Won't Be Long," for instance, became "Ca recommence" and "Hold Me Tight," "C'est fou, mais c'est tout." We even entered a local contest after rehearsing for weeks, and won — we were the only entrants.

I tell the story because so many of us went through it in one way or another, in those days. We all wanted to be in a band. It was a way out. It became in Québec what they now talk about as "L'ère des groupes" ("The Group Era"). Of course, the phenomenon was happening around the world in the mid-1960s, but in French Canada it reached proportions far exceeding the norm. It was a ghetto phenomenon.

It is also important to explain that, while poets like Félix Leclerc, Gilles Vigneault, Jean-Pierre Ferland, and Claude Léveillé — all of whom were known at least a little in English Canada — were writing powerful original folk-songs, the young, in the late 1950s and the 1960s, were listening either to English songs or to French translations of them. There were a lot of the latter. I knew them all and even wrote a few myself.

The famous Québec union leader Michel Chartrand once told me that the folk-singers had been important in the nationalistic revolution of the Québécois. He was right, but that wasn't obvious at all in the early 1960s. If anything, youth was drifting away from tradition and massively giving in to rock, and everything that came with it.

It was up to Robert Charlebois to really bridge the immense gap at the end of the decade of the Quiet Revolution. Sporting a "Canadiens" jersey and an afro, Charlebois was the first to successfully write and perform original French rock songs that captivated the young generation. "Lindbergh," a drug song if there ever was one, was his first big hit.

Charlebois could legitimately claim that he had given new life to French-Canadian songwriters. He made it possible to write rock songs without having to steal

American or British melodies. French was no longer the language of the "chansons à répondre."

His success touched other folk-singers, including the "chansonniers" like Vigneault who had been around for a while, but had not yet attained hero status among the baby-boom generation. The nationalists then latched on to the older *chansonniers* because they had become the symbols of what a proud Québec could do. They became living legends, and behaved as such.

Others emerged in the wake of Charlebois, bands like "Harmonium" and "Beau Dommage," the latter producing the incomparable singer-writer-composer Michel Rivard, probably the most talented performer ever to hit the stage in French Canada. And there is Michel Pagliaro, who is another multi-talented musician who performs in both languages.

In time — very quickly, in fact — the music of Québec's top performers became depoliticized. Even Charlebois tried his luck in English with songs like "It's Hallowe'en in Hollywood" and "Mister Plum." Although Michel Rivard wrote a beautiful song about French called "Le coeur de ma vie" ("The Heart of My Life") in the mid-1980s, the lyrics, far from a call for revolution, sound more like a quiet affirmation and an attempt at understanding between the two solitudes — he probably includes the Americans in his way of thinking when he writes: "It's not easy to live in the middle, when they lead the dance, when they are so numerous." And he speaks of "une langue de France aux accents d'Amérique" ("a language from France with an American accent"). Performance and success on the world stage have become more important to the new Québec performers than the mystical message of "la cause." They may have understood that the salvation of the nation starts with accomplishments that exceed its narrow-minded, navel-gazing politics.

Yet, for all their proud accomplishments on the music scene over the last thirty years, for all the cultural renaissance these musicians created within their borders, it is paradoxical that, today, three of Québec's megastars are Roch Voisine, Daniel Lavoie, and Céline Dion. Voisine is from New Brunswick, Lavoie is a Franco-Manitoban, and Dion is trying hard to make her living in English south of the border. Her talents earned her a chance to perform on the Academy Awards stage in 1992. But, in spite of her widely acclaimed talent and success, Dion had her own recent run-in with Québec's paranoid nationalist intelligentsia when she said, in July 1992, that she believed Québec separation would be "épouvantable" ("horrible"). She later felt she had to backtrack on her pro-Canada statement, and sheepishly said she should never have gotten involved in politics. She was afraid people in Québec would stop buying her records. Doesn't that sound a lot like being branded a "vendu"? It's a good example of the kind of moral pressure Québécois can be subjected to when they speak against the nationalist religion. Tough crowd.

And a comedian like André-Philippe Gagnon, from Québec, really became known in the province only after he made a stellar appearance on Johnny Carson's "Tonight Show." He's been packing them in ever since everywhere he goes.

Comedy also has always had a big place in French Canadians' hearts. It was not surprising that Montréal came up with the "Just for Laughs" festival — recently hosted by John Candy — in the 1980s, although it is true that Québécois seem to find any excuse for a festival or a carnival any time of year, from jazz in Montréal and Québec to the long-standing but little known "Festival Western de St-Tite," for Québec's cowboys. . . .

The greatest comedian Québec ever knew was assuredly one Olivier Guimond, whom English Canada sadly never got to know before his death more than a decade ago. Guimond had one of those faces that could make you laugh at the slightest twitch, and he was good at both slapstick comedy and stand-up routines. But for many years the province's intelligentsia rejected him, partly because they said he spoke French with an English accent, which, by the way, wasn't true. His mother, however, was an anglophone, and many believe that prejudiced critics against him. It didn't matter. The people fell in love with Olivier and, eventually, so did the critics. The most prestigious award for comedy in Québec is now named after him.

Guimond gave some of his best performances on Radio-Canada's traditional New Year's Eve show. While many anglophones are out celebrating with balloons, noise makers, and "Auld Lang Syne," even today, although habits are changing, French Canadians stay at home and gather around the TV to watch the annual "Bye-Bye" show, which pokes fun at everybody from politicians — a prime target — to current entertainment stars. The program is still an event that few people want to miss. When you do, you scramble to find a friend who videotaped it.

The Québécois, despite a very small market, have managed to develop a vibrant local TV industry fuelled lately by such writers as *La Presse* sports columnist Réjean Tremblay, author of "Lance et compte," the dramatic series about hockey that was not big in English Canada, and now of "Scoop," an incredibly popular se-

ries on journalism, and Lise Payette, former Parti Québécois minister and television talk-show host. Before
cablevision came along, there were also regions of Québec like Rimouski, the capital of the South Shore, where
for years the only TV station coming in was Radio-Canada.

The ultimate result is the creation of a society that
constantly talks and reads about itself in Québec, while
outside its borders, so-called Canadian values are being
promoted that have little to do with the French minority's aspirations and daily lives.

Québec newspapers predictably lead the charge in this
battle to resist the anglophone siege. After all, their own
commercial success depends on how many French francophones remain and how their numbers grow. Consequently, although most dailies in Québec have
traditionally been viewed as federalist with a Liberal
tint, any threat to the "nation" quickly produces unani-
mous anger and is turned into another "cause célèbre."
The most recent examples of this rare unanimity among
Québécois has to be the condemnation of Newfoundland
premier Clyde Wells in the Meech Lake debacle and, last
summer, the frontal attack on a Triple-E Senate.

The treatment of political news is almost always done
from a Québec angle. A deal among nine English premiers, for instance, turns into a gang-up on Québec in
the province's headlines.

It can be argued that newspapers anywhere in Canada
naturally tend to be parochial and serve their reader-
ship first, as the *Toronto Star* asks its reporters: "What
does it mean in Metro?" The difference in Québec, however, is that very little effort is made to even discuss in
the daily press what is going on in other Canadian regions. *Le Droit*, a French daily based in Ottawa but with

most of its 35,000 readers on the Québec side of the river, may be a notable exception. But it has more to do with its geographical location than a desire to bridge the gap between the two solitudes. Montreal's *Le Devoir*, a paper that, in spite of a circulation of fewer than 30,000, survives on its inflated prestige — paradoxically kept alive by English Canadians who feel it is the French equivalent of the *Globe and Mail* — and the aura of being a sacred institution, strives to remain the "national" newspaper. Only we're not too sure what "national" means anymore. Is the nation Canada or Québec? *Le Devoir*'s attempts at providing "national" coverage have been the subject of ridicule among the Québec media themselves: according to the jokes, a front page must include one story from Québec and another from Ottawa, whatever happens.

Even then, though, the syndrome of "us against them" more than often dictates the way news is treated. René Lévesque, for instance, made a lot of mileage out of repeated accusations of what he considered to be the *Gazette*'s unfair coverage of his government. Few members of the French media disagreed with the premier who could do no wrong. Québec reporters were then largely favourable to separation and, although management remained loyal to Canada, the bosses and editorialists were easily impressed, even intimidated, by the blind faith of the working press who had found the new religion. That commitment to Québec independence appears to have greatly subsided in the province's newsrooms and been replaced by a "nationalisme" that doesn't necessarily exclude Canada.

The massively unionized newsrooms have also retreated from the rabid militancy of the 1970s, which brought them huge salary increases and a four-day working week in many cases, to a more mellow attitude about labour relations. As elsewhere in Canada, reporters have realized there aren't that many jobs to go around anymore.

For the most part, Québec newspapers simply go with society's flow and the mood of the times. They flirted with socialism when the people were tempted by it; they were in favour of sovereignty when the people indicated they wanted to vote for René Lévesque. Québec journalists like to see themselves as leaders of the intelligentsia, but they follow the parade more often than they admit. In that sense, they are apolitical, with the crucial exception of the "defence of the race."

Newspapers are successful business ventures — otherwise Power Corporation's Paul Desmarais (*La Presse de Montréal, Le Nouvelliste de Trois-Rivières*, and *La Voix de l'Est de Granby*) and business tycoon Conrad Black (*Le Soleil de Québec, Le Quotidien de Chicoutimi*, and *Le Droit d'Ottawa*) wouldn't bother buying them up, and Pierre Péladeau wouldn't make *Le Journal de Montréal* and *Le Journal de Québec* the cornerstones of his empire.

There was even a time, in the mid-1970s, when Montréal boasted five French dailies — *La Presse, Le Journal, Le Devoir, Le Montréal-Matin* (a Union Nationale-sponsored tabloid that closed down), and *Le Jour* (a Parti Québécois creation that failed because of its perceived lack of objectivity).

For a people who apparently do not like to read, French Canadians have also supported quality magazines whose circulations defy the laws of publishing. *L'Actualité*, which recently went from monthly to bi-weekly, could be considered the top magazine in the country; the glossy monthly humour magazine *Croc*, which published its

150th edition in 1992, is in a class of its own and has nothing to compare it with in English Canada — certainly not *Frank*; another glossy called *Nous* reached a circulation of 80,000 in the late 1970s. It was considered a publishing miracle until it faded in the following decade, largely because of its clumsy attempts to be "light."

French Canadians also have nothing to be envious about when it comes to the "trash" tabloid press of the United States. They have plenty of their own, most of which have survived for a long time. *Allô Police* and *Photo Police* have survived on crime — and now sex — exploitation for decades, as *Echo Vedettes* and *Photo Vedettes* feed on the gossip from Québec's artistic community.

All this contributes to the creation of an environment in which the media constantly promote "la nation" because they flood the people with information about themselves, no matter how trivial or even repulsive.

It is very much the same in the book-publishing industry, where the "maisons d'édition," first and foremost, respond to the needs of the people. For instance, they will publish political books, but only about politicians they know will interest the people of Québec — Trudeau, Lévesque, etc. Even Brian Mulroney doesn't yet make the grade after eight years in power and overtures to his native province. Only icons sell.

Publishers have had incredible international successes in fiction, such as Gabrielle Roy's *Bonheur d'occasion* (*The Tin Flute*) or Yves Beauchemin's *Le Matou*. Classics like *Menaud Maître-Draveur*, *Maria Chapdelaine* and Thériault's *Agaguk* were a must-read in the schools.

The publishers, although saddled with the burden of having to charge outrageous prices for their books, have done very well. They have tackled the resistance to hardcover prices by switching to quality paperbacks, thus keeping prices more reasonable. And they have contributed greatly to Québécois' belief that they can do it on their own if only because they have a literature Lord Durham never thought they'd have.

But for all their stunning accomplishments, given the small market, French-Canadian artists have to compete not only within their own milieu, but against the more threatening invasion of English.

I laughed one day when I read a letter from an anglophone reader in an Ontario newspaper complaining about the fact that, in Québec, English Canadians were being forced to listen to radio in French only. It is true that there are some areas of Québec, like the North Shore, for instance, where only CBC is available to anglophones, just as in most of the rest of Canada francophones can only listen to Radio-Canada's affiliated stations.

But the most ironic part of it is that, for more than the last two decades, French radio stations have gone out of their way to play English music for one simple reason: ratings. So much so they had to be regulated by the CRTC not only for Canadian, but for francophone content. Tune in to any French private station in Québec's major centres and I guarantee that, with few exceptions, it will be a matter of minutes before you hear a familiar English tune.

It has been the radio stations' secret of survival. That, and talk shows. For some reason, Québécois seem to revel in phone-in shows where they can argue about anything from politics to sports to sex. The biggest battle for ratings takes place at noon in Montréal, when everybody tunes in to public-affairs programs.

Nothing, however, compares to the success of one André Arthur, known as "Le Roi Arthur," in Québec City, on the station he now owns, CHRC. The infamous Arthur probably holds the world's record for the number of libel suits he has been threatened with and is as famous for the loyalty of his audience as for his total disregard for objectivity. To give you an idea of his antics, let's just say that when Québec City hosted the Francophone Summit in 1987, in which many African heads of state participated, André Arthur callously labelled the event the "Cannibal Summit" — and got away with it.

In Québec, serious people have learned to shrug him off, while the ratings still follow him from one station to the other.

It didn't work in Montréal though. The biggest station in the province, CKAC, tried him out as a host a couple of years ago, but quickly gave up on him. He was simply too much for the "Métropole."

Which brings us to another Québec "distinctiveness": the rabid rivalry between the Big City, Montréal, and the "Vieille Capitale," Québec.

Other provinces have similar ongoing urban feuds — Calgary against Edmonton, Saskatoon against Regina. But none has one that appears so lop-sided, pitting a metropolis of almost three million people against a town of 300,000.

Some say the duel is more imagined than real, that Québec and Montréal's inhabitants like to keep it alive for the sake of it. It makes good material for comedians.

But it is more deep-rooted than that, and finds its origins in the days of New France, when Montréal was the centre for the fur-trade industry, and Québec the administrative capital.

When the British conquered New France in 1760, most

of the several hundred adventurers and businessmen who sought to profit from the conquest established themselves in what was to become the economic hub of the colony, Montréal. Meanwhile the government and the strongest French elite — including the powerful bishops — remained mainly in Québec City, where life seemed to go on relatively unchanged. That trend was not to be altered in the centuries to come as immigrants from abroad and French Canadians from big rural families naturally opted for Montréal rather than the relatively isolated provincial capital. They were going where the jobs were.

Time and evolution produced a society in Montréal that was largely French and blue-collar, dominated by an Anglo-Saxon establishment that for a long time remained isolated within its own walls. In Québec City, meanwhile, the social and governing French-Canadian elite remained relatively untouched, "pure" and in charge, the true keepers of the faith.

Even today, Québec City is a place outsiders love to visit, but few would want to live there. It is a closed society, with its aristocracy and its plebes. The lines are not easily crossed. And although visitors are welcome — especially since Québec relies so much on the tourism trade — and the walled old city is charming, you don't have to live there very long to realize the friendly atmosphere is a façade. Immigrants and outsiders have to assimilate or face being shut out. There are few anglophones, Jews, or even fluently bilingual people in Québec. Even the stubborn Irish have been absorbed. And that's the way the locals like it.

Sitting atop Cap Diamant, the fortress still looks as impregnable as ever. And although outnumbered, its proud defenders remain just as defiant and look down upon the cosmopolitan Montréalais as a lower breed of Québécois.

Of course, that's not the way they see it 140 miles up the St. Lawrence. The people of Montréal like to call Québec a "bourgade" — a pejorative term for village — and consider it to be an isolated outpost, far from everything that matters, with a winter two weeks too long "at both ends," the ultimate symbol of the province's isolation from the rest of the world.

To be fair, this is largely, if not strictly, a battle of elites. The ordinary folk don't care much about it, except perhaps when it comes down to one of the most important parts of Québec's culture: sports, mainly hockey.

Nothing epitomizes more the feud between Québec and Montréal than the rivalry that developed quickly between the Nordiques and the Canadiens.

It had been a long time coming. Ever since the Canadiens "stole" hall-of-famer Jean Beliveau from the "As de Québec" team of the old Senior League in 1953, the fans of "la bourgade" had been looking to get even.

They got some small comfort when the World Hockey League was formed and several top Canadiens jumped ship to the newly formed Nordiques.

But it really became a full-fledged battle when the WHA disbanded and the NHL absorbed four of its teams, including Québec.

The Nordiques pulled out all the stops to become the people's army, just as the Dallas Cowboys were called "America's Team." The battle didn't take place only on the ice. The breweries got into it, as they fought for television rights and a greater share of the market.

Stealing from the Parti Québécois' playbook, the Nordiques painted everything blue with fleur-de-lys and became the only team in the NHL to deliver the national anthem in French only. They went out of their way to recruit French-Canadian players and sought greater talent in Europe, mainly Czechoslovakia — with the Stastny brothers — when they couldn't find it at home.

While Montréalais called them mockingly the Nordiques "de Prague," Québec fans retaliated by dubbing the Canadiens the Montréal "Maroons" — from the name of the old Montréal team that assembled mainly English-speaking players at the beginning of the century.

Montréal could do nothing more but play the "Canada" card, appearing as the class team where linguistic differences didn't count as much as performance on the ice. But Québec had them worried. Especially in the early years when the rivalry was so intense it overtook politics as the number-one topic of discussion among French Canadians. In fact, it was politics, and religion too, all wrapped up in one powerful package, that brought out the best and the worst in the fans and the players themselves.

As Serge Savard, general manager of the Canadiens, told me in 1992: "They build themselves up by hitting on us. They use their status of small town against the big city."

Savard was rather serene about the whole thing, though. After all, the Canadiens, at that time, seemed to have won the popularity battle in the province. And it had more to do with their success at playing the game and the demise of the Nordiques as a team than with the media hype surrounding it. In fact, after a decade, the hottest rivalry in the NHL had waned considerably, simply because Québec couldn't compete.

But it is still there, like nationalism, just waiting for the next crisis to come to life again. In Montréal, they chuckled at the Eric Lindros affair, but they worried about how it would play with the people when the superstar rookie from Ontario who refused to play in the "Vieille capitale" said he wouldn't mind doing so in a Canadiens sweater.

That's because the last thing Montréal wants is to be perceived as the English team in Québec. The Canadiens did rejoice, however, when, at the same time as Québec was getting farther and farther embroiled in the Lindros mess, Savard traded francophone Stéphane Richer for anglophone Kirk Muller, and the Canadian-born player rejoiced publicly at the fact that playing for the Canadiens was a dream-come-true for him. They were being seen as the French, but "tolerant" alternative to the Nordiques. The nationalists who accept Canada.

Ironically, a few years earlier Québec-born "Super" Mario Lemieux had also refused at first to report to the Pittsburgh Penguins, and asked to be traded, only to surrender finally to the will of the league. Another French defeat.

If the world was watching, it must have wondered at our collective madness. All this fuss over hockey players. The sad reality is, though, that minorities naturally tend to identify so much with their athletes and their teams that their success or failure becomes an integral part of every individual's daily life. It affects his moods, his habits, his pride.

When the team loses, you lose. When they win, you win. Which explains why the CFL's Montreal Alouettes did not last. It wasn't only a matter of football not being a big French-Canadian game — it was because the team did badly. I know more than enough francophones who are avid National Football League fans. But cheering for a losing NFL team doesn't hurt as much, because it's American. You can cheer for a team, but the only real suffering comes if you put money on your own loser. The anger may still be there, but not the humiliation.

That also provides an explanation for the dwindling attendance at Expos games in the Olympic Stadium. In 1991, a market survey concluded that, in fact, Montréalais didn't go to baseball games because many of them thought the game dull. I don't believe it for a minute. French Canadians love and know baseball. It wasn't so long ago that they called them "Nos Expos, Nos amours." In their winning years, they broke attendance records.

Not that there were many French-Canadian — or even Canadian — players on the team. Claude Raymond was in his twilight years when he was traded to Montréal as a relief pitcher.

But the simple fact that the team was there, in Montréal, made each and every one of its players, whether white, black, American, or Latin, a member of the Québec family. Their successes and failures were linked to the greater good, "la cause." When they started to fail, it became too hard to take, because every loss was a personal one and hurt deeply.

It has always been this way for French Canadians. And those feelings of "appartenance," of being part of the team, of owning part of an athlete, naturally increase in intensity when the superstar happens to be one of your own.

Maurice Richard, Jean Beliveau, and Guy Lafleur are still among the few true heroes Québécois will always revere no matter what they do with their lives. Not only are they all French Canadians, but each individual represents a different set of values, of excellence, every Québécois aspires to.

Beliveau was the consummate gentleman, the calm, quiet, but powerful achiever who did everything with grace, without ever complaining or pushing people around.

Lafleur was the small-town boy who had to cope with big-city fame and struggled with it, emerging on top with sheer determination and talent. He wrecked his personal life, patched it up, and came back after a three-year retirement to play hockey again and give the crowd the chance to chant "Guy! Guy! Guy!" one more time.

If he'd been black and American, the cry would have been "Ali! Ali! Ali!"

But beyond Beliveau's grace and Lafleur's magical touch, is one Maurice Richard, who learned to play hockey in Montréal's Parc Lafontaine. Unpolished, uneducated, never rich, seldom happy, and totally irreverent in the face of authority, he represented their own kind to many French Canadians. His dark piercing eyes, which inspired such fear in opposing goalies; his Herculean strength, which defied the laws of physics; his explosive temper, which could explode into rage at the slightest provocation — all embodied the pent-up frustrations of an oppressed people from the ghettos, clawing its way up the hill to recognition and respect.

I met Maurice Richard in 1977. He had then been retired from the game for seventeen years and was known to be very bitter about hockey and the way the Canadiens had treated him.

Everybody knew the story about how Richard had slammed the door on the Forum, shortly after being offered a job in management where he found out very quickly he was just a figure-head, a marketing doll for the team. He also had a hard time swallowing the fact that he had been so poorly remunerated in his day, compared to other salaries of the day — and that was long before $1-million-a-year "Super Mario."

Richard booked the interview at an address in Montréal North, not exactly the thriving centre of the metropolis. The cab driver had a hard time finding it. As I recall, it was a TV repair shop, in the basement of a small building.

I went in thinking I was in the wrong place, but the worker who appeared to be in charge told me "Maurice" was indeed expected.

Richard showed up shortly afterwards and asked the same man if he could use his office for a half-hour or so. There was no discussion. But I couldn't help but feel sad for the man who had meant everything to my grandfather and so many other French Canadians.

There he was, a living legend, giving an interview in a basement TV repair shop. No wonder he was bitter.

I could tell he contained his true feelings throughout the conversation and, to be frank, when I looked into those eyes, I felt like so many other hockey players. I didn't want to mess with him.

I was too young to have seen Richard in his great years. But I understood, no matter the surroundings, why a people's heart had beaten in rhythm with his for so long, why French Canadians still talk about him the way Americans speak of "The Babe."

"Le Rocket" feared no one and nothing.

Years later, I would meet the great Montréal defence-man Doug Harvey, a few years before his death. And he would tell me how tough Richard was, how, as a rookie, he had punched out Harvey himself in the dressing-room after the team had performed on Maurice the traditional initiation rite of shaving his body bald. "He broke two of my teeth," said Harvey, who towered over Richard and wasn't one to be intimidated himself. He was simply impressed. He understood the love the people had for Richard.

There are some who say Québec's Quiet Revolution didn't really start in 1960. It happened five years earlier, when NHL president Clarence Campbell suspended Richard from the game, at the end of the season, depriving him of a scoring championship and leaving the Canadiens without him for the play-offs.

It followed a stick-swinging incident with the Boston Bruins' Hal Laycoe where Richard, willingly or not, ended up hitting official linesman Cliff Thompson twice — an unforgivable offence in hockey. But, as Chrys Goyens and Allan Turowetz point out in their excellent best-selling book on the Canadiens, *Lions in Winter*, it was rumoured in the six-team league at the time that there was a move afoot to "get" Richard. To this day nobody really knows or will admit whether "Le Rocket" knew who he was swinging at.

But, as the authors point out, the suspension showed that Campbell, as "a pillar of White Anglo-Saxon Protestant rectitude," was "proving once again he was totally out of touch with the French-speaking majority of the city in which he lived."

On St. Patrick's Day, 1955, the fans poured out of the Forum and onto Ste. Catherine Street in what turned out to be one of the worst riots Montréal has ever known.

The French wouldn't be pushed around anymore.

Despite the fact the unrest didn't accomplish the desired result of bringing Maurice Richard back on the ice, it taught the French Canadians a vital lesson. Even if they had only themselves to count on, they could still wreak a lot of havoc and shake the establishment into paying attention.

If Maurice Richard had the guts to fight, so did they. If he could come from nowhere to be the greatest at what he did, so could they.

Maybe it is true that that's where it all began — on a small patch of ice where French Canadians knew they could fight back.

Poutine and Mouton Cadet

≈ ≈ ≈

RESISTANCE CAN TAKE MANY FORMS — massive
public demonstrations, civil disobedience, urban guer-
rilla warfare, terrorism. Although the Québécois have
dabbled in them all, their struggle has been, like their
"revolution," a rather quiet one. Consciously or not, at
some point in their history, they decided to be different
simply in the way they go about their daily lives.

Many anglophones I know seem to suspect that their
francophone compatriots enjoy a special "joie de vivre,"
and many French Canadians believe it too. I think it is
more than a myth. We are, indeed, a looser bunch,
sometimes to the point of being irresponsible. The image
of French Canadians begins with their enjoyment of the
good life — food, wine, party, and song.

It has, for instance, long been seen as almost improper
in Montréal or Québec City to arrive at a discothèque or
piano bar before 10:30 or 11:00 p.m. Showing up before
that immediately brands you as an outsider or, worse,
an "Anglais."

It's not that people don't indulge before these late
hours. Happy Hours at Thursdays on Crescent Street

are still packed. But they usually start the evening by having dinner and go out dancing on a full stomach instead of a liquid diet of beer and shooters.

In fact, per capita, contrary to common belief in English Canada, Québécois (there aren't statistics for other francophone Canadians) consume only slightly more alcohol than English Canadians, 97 litres a year as compared to 95. There are, however, 492 establishments selling booze in Québec, compared to 160 in Ontario, thanks largely to the fact that beer, wine, apple cider, and various strange local derivatives, like blueberry apéritif, are sold in grocery stores. Which goes to show, I suppose, that although more controlled by the government, Ontarians drink just as much. They're just afraid to do it "officially," which would amount to making it too easy.

Québécois also like to consider themselves superior in the careful selection of what they drink. They believe they know and drink only good French wines, whereas the English are still at the "Baby Duck" level. They conveniently forget that not so long ago the preferred drink of their fathers was De Kuyper gin, known as "whisky blanc," stuff that could have passed for paint thinner, or "Caribou," a mixture of pure alcohol and cheap red wine that was a crowd favourite on sleigh rides and at carnivals. Liquor stores in Québec actually sell the wicked potion during the winter and make a killing during Carnival revelries.

It is only natural, however, that when you've had taverns open at 8:00 a.m. — for the guys coming off the night shift, of course — since time immemorial, and night clubs closing in the middle of the night — when they close at all — since the 1970s, drinkers do learn to pace themselves.

Jokes about drinking aside, an extensive poll done by *L'Actualité* in January 1992 — perhaps the most thorough ever — does establish clearly that Québécois put pleasure first. In answer to the question whether they put happiness before duty, 68 per cent of Canadians from other provinces chose duty, whereas 51 per cent of the people of Québec — including anglophones — chose happiness. This represents a fundamental difference in their approach to life, perhaps more important than any other facet of Québécois life — language, the Civil Code, etc. — used by politicians and opinion makers to explain the distinct quality of society there.

What *L'Actualité* didn't report was that there are sharp class divisions in Québec, as elsewhere. Those who have attained a higher level of education and general culture often look down on the less-educated masses that earned French Canadians the reputation of a people who think a Pepsi and a Mae West (a chocolate cookie) make a great lunch.

There is a word unique to the French-Canadian vocabulary — you won't find it in a dictionary sanctioned by l'Académie française — used to describe the pleasures of less-worldly people: when you hear a francophone say something is "quétaine" (pronounced "K-Ten," as in "K-Tel"), it is a major insult to someone's taste and culture.

We are talking here about the "poutine" culture. If you don't know by now, "poutine" consists of french fries smothered with melted cheddar cheese and drowned in a thick brown gravy. I've never had it, but I confess my kids swear by it. As the legend goes, it was invented in the Eastern Townships town of Plessisville — or so swears long-time Telemedia reporter Yves Bellavance, a Sherbrooke native who, like everybody in Sherbrooke, knows everything.

You don't admit to eating poutine if you consider yourself a member of the educated and cultured elite. Many, of course, do it secretly.

Actually, "guedilles" came before "poutine," but never really caught on. What's a "guedille"? When I was a kid, it referred to stuff running out of your nose in winter. But as a delicacy, it's made of french fries — what else? — in a hot-dog bun with cole slaw. Not messy or greasy enough to become popular.

What is misunderstood in English Canada, though, is that the Québécois know perfectly well that poutine, guedilles, and Pepsi are "déclassés." In a strange way, they like to laugh about themselves. They enjoy the attention and the befuddlement of outsiders, as tribesmen would chuckle at a city boy who won't eat goats' eyeballs. After all, for the Québécois, it fits perfectly with the mentality that you are free to enjoy yourself any way you can as long as you don't impose your tastes on others.

The more cultured set, of course, which I call the "club des parvenus," seeks contentment in pricier, more sophisticated delicacies. A *parvenu* is what most successful French Canadians are today — with the few exceptions of those who are descendants of doctors, lawyers, or colonial seigneurs who stayed on after the Plains of Abraham.

To check out Québec's upper culinary class, just drop by "Le Mas des Oliviers," a restaurant on Bishop Street in Montréal, during lunch hour any day of the week. You'll be lucky to find a place to sit at the bar. The city's powerbrokers are torn between it and the Ritz-Carlton, but "Le Mas" has a cosier atmosphere. It's the same in

Québec City, where top bureaucrats and politicians often disappear at 12:00 noon and go settle the world's problems in a more pleasant setting. I must say I am told the trend is changing in the Old Capital, though, as the New Morality has thinned the ranks of the diehards who like to mix business with pleasure.

The same is happening in Ottawa, where the so-called French table at the National Press Club is much more subdued than it used to be when I arrived on The Hill thirteen years ago. We still, however, laugh louder, get into more animated discussions to the point where observers think we're fighting, and hang around longer than most other patrons.

Maclean's columnist Allan Fotheringham once remarked, while walking by our table, that we were the only people in the country who knew how to eat. We like that reputation, even though to a growing number of others it is the equivalent of irresponsibility and frivolity. As Jean-Pierre Ferland's song goes: "We'd rather kill ourselves living than live our deaths."

That is not to say that I haven't met anglophones who enjoy good — or is it bad? — living as much as French Canadians do. As I've said before, I've been lucky that way. But the difference lies in the collective acceptance of such behaviour. As the pollsters in *L'Actualité* pointed out: our attitude borders on delinquency.

It's not even that all or even a majority of French Canadians overindulge in the pleasures of life. In fact, the CROP poll showed surprisingly that they go out to restaurants less often than Anglo-Canadians do — although, when they do, they spend more. Québécois actually like to stay home and watch TV, and are greater "pantouflards" ("people in slippers") than they would have you believe.

But their tolerant attitude towards what may be perceived as excess elsewhere in the country goes to the very heart of who they are. The pollsters for *L'Actualité* were shocked to find out that, whereas pundits over the years have seen their society as one that puts the collective interest before the individual, Québécois are actually very individualistic in their approach to life.

I could have told them that. We were raised not to trust many strangers and to pick our friends carefully, especially those of our own cultural and linguistic background. How many times did I hear from my parents and others in a position of authority: "French Canadians like to take the wool off each other's backs." We were taught first and foremost not to trust our own. It was common wisdom in French-Canadian society that you had to beware first of those you believed to be your friends or natural allies. It may have something to do with some kind of fear of "collaborateurs," as happened in France after the Nazi invasion. And there may be a lot of similarities with the situation in France, where after the liberation, everyone claimed to have been a member of the resistance. Again, it is the lot of a minority to worry that the one who smiles at you today could stab you in the back for a few pieces of gold tomorrow. Whatever it is, we were taught at a young age that the most pernicious human weakness of all was jealousy, and that our own people would go out of their way to feed the demon. We learned never to flaunt our successes too much, for fear it would only encourage the envious to bring us down. Poet and folk-singer Félix Leclerc captured the essence of this French-Canadian trait when he wrote in one of his earlier hits: "Le plaisir de l'un c'est le voir l'autre se casser le cou" ("One finds pleasure in seeing the other break his neck").

We are drastically different from anglophones, for instance, in the way we deal with neighbours. I can't remember my parents socializing with our neighbours; I can't recall any neighbour ever being invited to our home. Their children were welcome, because they played with or babysat us. But the parents didn't mix.

A recent story in *L'Actualité* described the experience of a Montréalais who was transferred by his company to Toronto's multicultural community of North York. "The neighbours on Beachwood Street were waiting for me with coffee and sandwiches. Later they invited us over for tea and they helped us renovate our house." When he moved back to the Montréal suburb of St-Lambert, his neighbours called the police because they thought there was too much activity on the street. French Canadians do not accept outsiders easily, and will be wary of anything they do — including moving in their furniture — until they're assured that their world isn't threatened.

Cops. Québécois are as ambivalent about them as they are about their political options. They rank way up on the list of trusted professionals — 78 per cent of Québécois show confidence in them — but this figure is still 10 per cent below that in the rest of the country. Also, it is not uncommon for Québécois to refer pejoratively to "chiens" ("dogs") and "boeufs" ("bulls") when talking about them.

This has a lot to do with the Québécois' visceral rejection of all authority. As Environics pollster Michael Adams put it, the Québécois are saying: "We have had enough of being told what is permissive and what isn't."

Many experts believe this is the natural reaction of a people who have been told what to do, first by the clergy, then by their politicians, and now, more and more, by their business leaders.

I disagree slightly. Though often pliant, we French Canadians were never totally submissive under the yoke of the Catholic church. If anything, religion gave us the perfect way out. We could swear, steal, have sex out of wedlock, or just be all-around bad, but if we went to confession and said a few Hail Marys as penance, we were brand new again. It was clever of the Catholic church to give us such an outlet. It was actually possible to regret a sin and still repeat it.

True, that's not to say there weren't moments of embarrassment, even fear. Not all priests let you off easy. But big sinners got to sort out those who didn't seem to care about your awful conduct from the more righteous ones who would lecture you and sentence you to a couple of rosaries.

Another important point is that, from the early days of the colony, there was always animosity between the church and the "coureurs de bois," the renegade fur traders and adventurers of New France. The priests didn't approve of the wild ways of the coureurs de bois, especially when they came back from their treks in the wilderness thirsty for *whisky blanc* and hungry for women.

The clergy could not always control the influence these free spirits had on the rest of the population, although they tried, as when they moved a group of Mohawks converted to Catholicism farther away from Montréal to keep them from drunkenness and rowdiness as a result of contact with the coureurs. They offered the Mohawks land — in Oka.

In the general population, the defiance of church rule, if not of its clergy, was perhaps more discreet, but nonetheless always present in a society made up largely of people who had fled the oppressive regime of the old country.

French Canadians do not break the law any more than do their English counterparts. In fact, the criminal statistics compare rather favourably. But they like to make small transgressions, perhaps another vestige of their resistance to authority.

My former *Le Droit* editor used to marvel at the fact that Ontarians were so disciplined, they actually parked between the white lines in a parking lot. "You go to Québec and cars are all over the place," he said.

Another colleague couldn't understand why anglophone drivers tended to wait patiently at a red light in the middle of the night when no cars were coming and nobody was around.

If you really want to experience this form of mild disobedience, just drive through Montréal some day, any day. If you survive the local drivers — a bunch of maniacs who all think they're Gilles Villeneuve — watch the pedestrians. "Don't walk," in any language, doesn't mean a thing to them. When they get to an intersection, they cross it, sometimes without even looking for oncoming cars.

Québécois don't like to impose too many laws on themselves. For years they had the worst record in Canada of traffic deaths involving the abuse of alcohol, but they were slow in legislating against drunk driving. When the provincial government imposed the use of car safety belts, short-lived Union Nationale leader Roch La Salle campaigned against it. It didn't help him much, but of all the unrealistic things he had to promise this may have been the most popular element of his platform.

While we're on the subject of authority, how about permissiveness and sex?

A Montréal friend of mine was once called an "oversexed Frenchman" by another man in a Western Canadian bar. He took it as a compliment. The CROP poll asked several tough trick questions about the matter. Rather than asking a general question about sexual tolerance in terms of permissiveness and orientation, the poll sought opinions about specific situations.

The toughest, certainly, was the question asking parents if they would mind if their children had a homosexual teacher. While 51 per cent of other Canadians found the idea repugnant, 63 per cent of Québécois said they wouldn't mind. If that is not "distinct" I don't know what is.

It shouldn't be that surprising, however. Québécois have long had homosexuals in positions of respect and authority and haven't flinched. The most obvious example is likely former PQ minister Claude Charron, who became nationally famous after he was caught shoplifting a sports jacket at Eaton's when he was still in René Lévesque's cabinet.

Everybody who was anybody in Québec, including the people who elected him, knew Charron was gay. Tall tales about the minister's sexual exploits were regular fodder for the political rumour mill. Yet it was never brought up in the press or used against him in any way. It probably would have backfired. Charron's book *Désobéir* (*To Disobey*) was a best-seller in the province, and he is now a successful television public-affairs show host.

Pierre Bourgault, one of the province's first separatist

leaders and widely considered to be its most eloquent orator, was also known to be gay long before he admitted it to *L'Actualité* in the early 1980s.

As far as I know, only one other place in the rest of the country comes close to this kind of permissiveness — Vancouver. And, curiously, as *L'Actualité*'s poll showed, the people of British Columbia are as "distinct" from other Canadians as Québécois are, which may explain, at least in part, why federal NDP MP Svend Robinson was re-elected after professing his gay orientation.

Sex of all kinds — in clubs and films and on the airwaves — is an accepted phenomenon in Québec. Pornographic movies are shown regularly on private networks — usually on Friday or Saturday nights. In the late 1970s a Hull TV station had to face charges in an Ottawa court for airing such material. Although the station was located on the Québec side of the river, the Crown contended that it could be charged in Ontario because the signal was readily available there. Strangely enough, it was the most popular French program among anglophones in the Nation's Capital.

Which probably explains why Hull's "xxx" video-rental stores have an Ontario membership as big as their own.

It is also perfectly acceptable to discuss sex on radio in Québec. At one point in the 1980s a Montréal station had a daily afternoon program that dealt only with that subject.

Some of Québec's first locally successful movies were also borderline pornographic. The biggest hit was a sex comedy featuring established actors called *Deux femmes en or* (*Two Women Made of Gold*). The story line deals with two housewives who decide they're going to have sex with every man who knocks on their door.

They end up in court and are pardoned by a judge played by none other than fiery union leader Michel Chartrand, who was well-known for his hatred of the justice system. Having him play the part was just another way of attacking the established order, to the crowd's delight.

And, of course, even more sophisticated films such as Denys Arcand's *The Decline of the American Empire* deal with sex openly, if a bit more cerebrally.

Other revealing numbers from *L'Actualité*'s poll:

- 46 per cent of Québécois adults accept that adolescents aged fifteen or sixteen engage in sexual relations, as opposed to only 30 per cent of other Canadians;
- 68 per cent of Québécois believe marriage is an important institution, as opposed to 92 per cent of other Canadians;
- 79 per cent of Québécois believe having an extra-marital affair is a very serious infraction, while 89 per cent of other Canadians think so.

Although this is not a picture of total permissiveness, it does underline basic attitudes that are sharply different collectively from those of English Canadians. The most revealing number has to be the gap between the 68 per cent of Québécois who believe marriage to be an important institution and the 92 per cent of English Canadians who do. This is an unmistakable sign of a general respect for individualism; after releasing themselves from the church's shackles three decades ago, the Québécois refuse to have a set of rules imposed on them. It also indicates a disregard for responsibility and a desire to be free to make choices and change directions throughout one's life. It is a commonly accepted principle for French Canadians that money is better spent while you are alive "because you won't take it with you."

The search for pleasure often goes hand in hand with the quest for beauty — the ultimate self-satisfaction. It should therefore come as no surprise that Québec City's and Montréal's women are collectively considered to be the best dressed in the country — by both anglophones and francophones, as far as I can tell.

What we rarely hear or read about, though, is the fact that men in the province are just as concerned about their appearance.

Clothes, of course, cost money, but *L'Actualité*'s poll confirms this is not a major concern of Québécois. Money spent on appearance and social status is a valid investment. Seventy-one per cent of Québécois, as opposed to 51 per cent of other Canadians, think that buying something new — including clothes — is one of the greatest pleasures in life. It's not that anglophones don't appreciate new things, but the first question they tend to ask is: "How much does it cost?"

That does not appear to be a major consideration for the Québécois who, for instance, still shy away from "no-name" products at the grocery store because "cheaper" means "inferior in quality" to them. A majority of them want to retire by age fifty-five, to enjoy life (what else?), but nobody knows where they'll get the money. Numbers from *L'Actualité*'s poll show that 50 per cent more Torontonians invest in retirement savings than do Montréalais. However, the people of Montréal believe in luck, as they buy 40 per cent more lottery tickets than do Toronto inhabitants. It may have something to do with those "indulgences" the church used to give us as a ticket to heaven.

Legendary mayor Jean Drapeau had understood in his own way that "people want glamour." "When I campaigned on more public housing, I lost," he would say. So he gave the Montréalais a subway, Expo 67, and the Olympics. As they so often do, the Québécois had their fun and paid later.

All this being said, Québécois are also distinct in other, less flattering ways. The CROP poll showed they generally don't take part in community or volunteer work, prefer pollution over the closing of a factory, are still not very open to the world or travel abroad — with the exception of "la Floride" — and don't read books.

The last-named finding is assuredly a fair reflection of the crisis in education and general culture I referred to earlier. The numbers are, in fact, staggering. Thirty-seven per cent of Québécois admitted not having read a single book over the previous six months, as opposed to 15 per cent in other provinces. The men fared much worse than women, at 47 per cent compared to 28 per cent. On average over a six-month period, a Québécois reads 5.7 books, as opposed to 9.2 in the rest of the country.

Predictably, they don't do very well when their knowledge of foreign personalities and their professions is tested. Forty-six per cent of French Québécois knew who Idi Amin Dada was, but only 13 per cent identified Rudolph Nureyev as a ballet dancer, compared to 38 per cent in other provinces. Only 22 per cent knew Ingmar Bergman was a filmmaker, compared to 51 per cent in English Canada. After almost tying with them on Idi Amin, they beat the other Canadians on only two questions out of eight, as 50 per cent correctly identified France's Philippe Noiret as an actor against only 3 per cent of other Canadians, while 14 per cent of them knew that Gabriel García Márquez was a writer, as opposed to 6 per cent in English Canada. Interestingly enough, though, 16 per cent of Anglo Québécois knew the answer to the latter. Any remaining doubts about the two solitudes?

As for the attraction of Florida, you have to travel to North Miami and cruise "the Biscayne" strip to understand how much Québécois have taken over. Walking into a club, I could have sworn I was in a Baie Comeau piano bar, as the show as much as the audience carried on in "joual."

I met a lot of Québécois who have made Florida another home, some year-round, others for the winter. And not just retired couples, though there are plenty of them. They have their own local associations and they insist on being served in French in stores — with more success than they would have in Winnipeg.

But I also met quite a few young people who just got in a car one day and headed south. They have no working visas, but they find jobs, on construction sites mostly, since, apparently, American contractors like French-Canadian labour. They're more reliable than the locals, I was told.

When spring comes along, they lock up their trailers and head north for the summer and another blue-collar job. They head back to Florida before the first snow falls. To them, it is the perfect, independent way of life. Some have been doing it for years and still don't speak English fluently; but in Miami they have their friends, their place, the sun, and a job.

Anglo Québécois compare favourably with their French compatriots in several ways. They travel to more different destinations, they are better informed about foreign affairs, and take part in more community activities (20 per cent more). When it comes to their attitudes towards life and pleasure, they have reached a level of tolerance comparable to that of the Québécois, although they have a slightly greater sense of civic and social responsibility and a tendency to spend less when they eat in restaurants.

In that sense, they have been influenced by, if not assimilated into, the Québec mainstream and are themselves very different from other English Canadians — if only because they are among the most fluently bilingual people in the country. As an anglophone former Montréalais told me after going back to the city for a holiday: "Even the anglos there don't understand the rest of Canada." Perhaps it is true that those who didn't want to change with the Quiet Revolution have left.

As a Franco-Ontarian, I can say that we too have been influenced by the majority. As Liberal MP for Ottawa-Vanier Jean-Robert Gauthier once said: "We are hybrids." And although I consider most of my natural instincts and values to be more Québécois than anything else, I have to admit to a much greater interest in the other culture in what I read, in the movies and TV programs I watch, and, of course, in my work for an anglophone newspaper.

One of the thorniest issues raised about the Québécois recently has been that of racism and the impression being spread in English Canada that Québec is a more racist society than others. I have already described what they taught us in school. And, of course, in his controversial article in *The New Yorker* and his subsequent book, *Oh Canada, Oh Quebec!*, Mordecai Richler caused a sensation in both English and French Canada with his assertion that Jews were outcasts in Québec. All in all, at first glance, it doesn't make a very pretty picture.

Let's start with a current question, that of the Native Canadians our textbooks used to identify as "savages." I have seen racism with my own eyes in the remote village of Natashquan on the North Shore, the birthplace of fiery nationalist singer-composer Gilles Vigneault. One of his first hit songs was called "Jack Monoloi," and had to do with a local Indian who committed suicide after his white girlfriend was sent away to a convent because a white girl with a Native was unthinkable. A beautiful, sad song, and unfortunately too close to reality.

I went to Natashquan in 1985 as an advance man for Brian Mulroney, who was scheduled to travel there to announce the building of a long-awaited road linking the village to civilization. The local white authorities suggested holding a barbecue for the occasion, but when I asked if they would invite the Indians from the nearby reserve, they said that would not be wise because "the Indians would eat everything." If the prime minister's brother, Gary, hadn't been there to settle me down, I would have cancelled everything, including the road. In the end, the Natives were invited, but I was shocked to see them standing at the back of the crowd, far from the whites. They knew they were not welcome.

But is that really different from the fate of Indians in Western Canada? Is it worse than my experience in a restaurant in Regina, where a waitress explained that the reason there were German shepherds in the police cars was that "they really don't like them Injuns

Then, of course, there are the recent events at Oka and Châteauguay, and the ugly scenes of French-Canadian mobs stoning the Natives. Try to imagine a bunch of gun-toting terrorists, unilingual French, blocking the Don Valley Parkway in Toronto for a couple of months and see how English Canadians would react.

All this to say that the Québécois may not be any better in their intolerance of Natives, but their current attitudes stem largely from the recent confrontation that lasted too long and caused many people to lose their sense of balance. The Oka-Châteauguay confrontation, mixed up, as it was, with gambling and cigarette-smuggling interests that confused the issue as much as the extension of the Oka Golf Club, found its roots in the fact that the Québécois had taken the Natives for granted for too long. They were happy to buy their cheap cigarettes and spend money at their bingo games, but no one in Québec society ever stopped to think that the reserves were more than an aboriginal ghetto, and that it was, in fact, Indian land they were building roads and bridges on. The problem is so hard for Québécois to confront today because in their minds it never existed. It is a cruel irony that they are caught in a situation where they now have to try to understand the needs and aspirations of a minority they unwittingly oppressed.

There is no question that we have a long way to go, and Québec Natives being mainly English by choice, the linguistic issue will no doubt cloud the debate and slow attempts at reconciliation for some time.

As for the Jewish community, it is certainly true that anglophone Jews have made more efforts to bridge the gap between themselves and francophones than vice versa. And in the course of my research for this book I discovered that there is still rampant anti-semitism, or, at the very least, profound distrust of things Jewish, in Québec. It is not organized and blatant anymore, but the feeling is deep-rooted, and you can feel the exas-

peration of French Québécois everytime you bring up
the subject. Many simply see Jews as provocateurs who
try to excite compassion for themselves by complaining
about racism at the drop of a hat.

Ironically, if there is any truth to this, B'nai B'rith is
not very different from the St-Jean-Baptiste Society,
which goes ballistic at the slightest insulting comment
or derogatory observation coming from English Canada.
"Deux poids, deux mesures": the old double standard.

Francophones like to defend themselves by saying they
are not the ones who banned the Jews from their country clubs and universities. The wasps did that. True.
But the wasps didn't have school manuals calling the
Jewish society "deicidic," as far as I know. They simply
quietly acted on their prejudice.

But my sense is that the Québécois still have a long
way to go before they stop being wary of the Jews allying
themselves with the English minority against them. It's
at least partly because of the orthodoxy of the new religion of nationalism: If you're not with us, you're against
us.

Another frightening prospect is the looming problem
of the black population in Montréal, where francophone
immigrants from Haiti are clashing with anglophones
from Jamaica and the United States, and the police do
little to improve the situation. There have been ugly
racial incidents — white police shooting blacks, whites
refusing to ride in cabs driven by Haitians — but similar
incidents have occurred in English Canada, notably in
Toronto.

L'Actualité's 1992 poll claimed that the Québécois
actually showed greater tolerance towards immigrants
to their province because 72 per cent wished to assimilate them into their society, as opposed to only 55 per

cent of other Canadians. But what does "assimilate" mean — does it mean tolerance? That they want them to feel at home or that they want to turn them into images of themselves? As *L'Actualité* points out, "The linguistic debate probably greatly influences those results."

It must be said, however, that I was told by a senior official in the federal Department of Immigration that their in-house polls show a greater tolerance of immigrants in Québec than in most other regions of the country.

Perhaps there has been a breakthrough. In 1989, when the federal government decided to expel many Turks who had sought refugee status in Québec, the French media came massively to the Turks' defence and unsuccessfully tried to keep them in the country.

Racism, distrust of English Canadians, ignorance of foreign affairs: all these traits are significant, because they indicate the Québécois' besieged mentality, their age-old fear of losing language and identity, of being swamped by the Other. It may seem absurd to English Canadians who feel the Québécois won their cultural battle in the 1960s, but I think it is this old fear, rather than any true hatred of other ethnic groups, that has produced the perceived racist tendencies. In the end, I think few French Canadians are brought up today hating or despising one collectivity or another. I don't even think they hate those "maudits Anglais," except that many of them, on their territory, see the use of French as a show of respect. Our constant constitutional bickering has also confused the issue greatly. Yet, just as many are ready to cater to English-speaking people, and I think the horror stories of Anglo-Canadians being insulted in the streets of Montréal are greatly exaggerated.

If anything, I usually hear the contrary from unilingual English friends who travel to the province.

Finally, as a kicker to close this chapter, I couldn't let this one go by. If you still have doubts about Québec's distinctiveness, here is an unassailable statistic for you: although the Québécois constitute only about one-quarter of the country's population, they drink 54 per cent of the tomato juice consumed in Canada.

Go figure.

How We See You

๛ ๛ ๛

THOUGH IT HAPPENED IN THE LATE 1970s, I remember it as if it were yesterday. When the front-page editorial appeared, we in the newsroom at *Le Droit* looked at each other in puzzlement. What was a "Protestant work ethic" anyway?

As the story went, it meant working harder, a practice French Canadians should adopt to better their attitude and improve their chances of success in the real world.

In typical fashion, we laughed heartily about it. If that meant we had to become more like the English, we'd rather be lazy and poor, as long as the little money we had was spent on fun.

How often over the years have I seen francophones recoil in horror from social attitudes they call "des patentes d'Anglais," a phrase that translates roughly as "English idiosyncrasies."

Usually — if not always — it refers to something that can't be very enjoyable, like drinking tea and eating cookies at a given hour of the day — although the practitioners make a great effort to make it look as if they're actually having a ball.

To most French Canadians, anglophones, by and large, form a society that has collectively lived in the closet. Personally, I have been blessed to work in a journalistic environment that produced anglophone exceptions to this stereotype. But, even in my privileged milieu, general attitudes to life, work, and duty often point to a society that, compared to the francophones', lives in a strait-jacket from which it escapes only behind closed doors.

Far be it from me to claim that French society is perfect. In fact, the French-Canadian attitude of living for the day and being on your own has created a society that sometimes doesn't seem to give a damn about important things beyond three-hour lunches and a few good bottles of Bordeaux, chased with a double calvados and espresso coffee.

The French Canadians' carefree and individualistic attitudes have certainly been more apparent, even blatant, since the Catholic church became irrelevant and the Québécois deliberately set out to emphasize "la différence."

Language had a lot to do with it, as more and more educated francophones turned to Europe and the long-lost mother country to seek their identity, whereas in English Canada the natural tendency was to look to the United States for cultural fulfilment, all the time being terrified of its influence.

That is not to say French Canadians isolate themselves from their southern neighbours. Quite the contrary, historically they have warmed to the Americans and their culture far more than to English Canadians, who were perceived as the invaders and oppressors.

I was brought up, for instance, to cheer for the New York Yankees and their heroes — Mickey Mantle, Whi-

tey Ford, and Roger Marris — with as much respect as
I showed the Montréal Canadiens. Former Québec premier Maurice Duplessis, the incarnation of isolationism,
spent his yearly holiday attending the World Series. Until Pierre Trudeau came along, the only politician we
ever had any deep admiration for was John Kennedy.
We knew more about him than about Mackenzie King,
John A. Macdonald, John Diefenbaker, Lester B. Pearson, or even Sir Wilfrid Laurier.

An incredible number of French-Canadian families —
including my own — have long-lost relatives in New
England. In my childhood, I heard my parents and
grandparents speak of Boston as some sort of second
haven for francophones — all of whom, of course, can't
speak a word of French today.

Just watch an NFL football game and check out the
French names on the backs of the jerseys. You'll be
surprised. Think of quarterbacks like Bobby Hebert or
Jack Trudeau. Think of baseball greats like Leo Duro-
cher or even ex-Yankees pitcher Ron Guidry, a Loui-
siana Cajun whose unilingual French grandfather once
said in an interview he didn't like his grandson's baseball team much because it was a little too English for
his taste.

Quite a few of these Americans with French names
are the descendants of Québec immigrants who left their
homeland by the hundreds of thousands in the early
part of the century to seek fortune or, at the very least,
employment south of the border. Some studies have
suggested the number of French Canadians would be
double what it is today had it not been for those
massive migrations.

All this to say that francophones don't perceive Americans as a threat, as they do English Canadians. Rather

they are good hosts who offer cheap beer; inexpensive trailerpark holidays in North Miami or on the ocean front in Old Orchard, Maine; tolerate the use of French on their territory; and let the French fly the fleur-de-lys — although that has ruffled some patriotic feathers at times.

Francophones, by and large, see only the positive side of the red, white, and blue giant. The American values of individual freedom, entrepreneurship, and success achievable for all have often clouded their vision of the ugly side of the monster, and the fact that, had it not been for the British, chances are they'd be American and speaking English today.

Many were understandably shocked when New York State turned on them in the winter of 1992 by cancelling a $17-billion contract with Hydro-Québec. Few stop to consider that their nationalistic or sovereigntist attitudes don't play too well on Wall Street or in the White House, where the history of North American francophones is something that belongs to folklore, as in Louisiana, the poorest state in the Union.

French Québécois are more open to American television culture, for instance, than they are to English-Canadian programming. In fact, the thorough study done by *L'Actualité* and published in January 1992 showed that, although English Canadians didn't care much about French TV, they still appeared more interested in learning about Québec culture than Québécois are in discovering the other Canada.

Just flick through daytime television in Québec and find these poor man's versions of American game shows like "Wheel of Fortune" ("La roue de fortune") or "Jeopardy" (in French, guess what? "Jeopardy"). Yet the French never heard of "Don Messer's Jubilee" in its heyday, few know about "Front Page Challenge," even fewer about classics like "The King of Kensington" or "The Beachcombers." Even if they did, chances are few would identify with such productions that are so English Canadian they are more alien to the Québécois than "Dallas."

L'Actualité's wide-ranging CROP poll confirms this as it shows only 8 per cent of French Québécois watch television in the other language. English Canadians fare predictably worse, as only 2 per cent of them tune in to French on TV. I was honestly surprised by those numbers. Not so much the numbers pertaining to anglophones watching French TV: actually, I think the 2 per cent figure is high. But I really thought more French Québécois watched English programming. A Franco-Ontarian — Ottawa — distortion.

There have been some recent successes for English-Canadian productions: "Anne of Green Gables," for instance, captured 20 per cent of Québec's audience, as opposed to only 15 in English Canada.

But then there have been dismal failures, like "Lance et compte," a series that was deliberately made in both languages — with no translation. It ended up highlighting the great divide between the two cultures it was supposed to unite under the perennial Canadian unifying theme of hockey. In 1988, in Québec, "Lance et compte" captured 40 per cent of the audience, whereas only 0.5 per cent of English Canadians watched the show before it was taken off the air and out of production in English. It may have had something to do with the fact that the hockey team featured in the series closely resembled the Québec Nordiques and their uniforms were plastered with fleur-de-lys.

L'Actualité quotes Québec poet Hélène Filion, a Margaret Atwood expert, as saying: "The Québécois don't really want to discover the other culture." The numbers from the publishing industry are even more revealing: English-Canadian book publishers have translated and printed far more translations of French work than Québec's editors have done of English since the Quiet Revolution. "As an example," notes *L'Actualité*, "from 1974 to 1983 English publishers have marketed seven anthologies of French Canadian short stories and plays," but no such initiatives have been taken in Québec. "Ask them who Robertson Davies is. France knows more about Margaret Atwood, who was a guest of president François Mitterrand, than French Québécois do."

Perhaps this lack of interest in all things English Canadian is attributable to the old stereotype of "les Anglais" as being boring prudes. Québécois, for instance, have got "partying" down to a science. Typically, they believe English Canadians are ignorant of this hedonistic art and turn into savages when they unleash their pent-up feelings to try and have fun.

For one thing, "les Anglais" can't drink. "We see them when they come here on student exchanges," says a Chicoutimi man. "They go crazy. They drink like lushes. We teach our kids self-discipline." Hmm.

You don't have to go to Chicoutimi to hear Québécois complain about the anglophones' lack of self-restraint when they are under the influence. Just go across the bridge from Ottawa to Hull on a Friday or Saturday night, after the bars have closed in Ontario and there's still a solid two hours of partying to be had on the Québec side. A lot of the violence and drunkenness late at night is blamed on les Anglais from Ottawa. So much so that the Hull police brutally cracked down on the revellers in the summer of 1992 with a policy called "Tolerance

Zero." The result: of fourteen people arrested one night, for instance, thirteen were Ontarians; the other was an American.

Inevitably, when they travel to other provinces (often more by necessity than by choice), the Québécois will bitch about three things: the silly drinking hours, the lousy food in restaurants, and the "drab" appearance of the women. Most times, it is a reflex action that doesn't necessarily correspond to reality. The French simply don't feel at home in cities and towns where everything is done in English, and tend to react by acting superior.

I take this observation from many, many hours on the road with groups of journalists from the two solitudes.

"Les maudits Anglais," of course, are fair game. It is not considered racist to put them down collectively, although I believe French Canadians do it more out of habit than conviction. After all, many English Canadians still refer to us casually as "frogs" and "pea soupers."

On that last point, the Québécois didn't think it was very brilliant of Franco-Ontarians in the 1970s to try to cope with the anglophone backlash in the province by wearing T-shirts and buttons saying "I'm a frog, kiss me." It was seen as an Uncle Tom reaction rather than an attempt to bridge the cultural gap.

French Canadians, especially the Québécois, see English Canada as a monolithic society — one that is out to get them at every turn. This is, of course, not true, but the perception contributes greatly to reactions like the rejection of the Meech Lake Accord, in which nine premiers out of ten agreed with the idea of a "distinct society," but Québec still felt it had lost another battle to the English. French Canadians strongly suspect that anglophones will accept them only when they become more anglophone themselves; hence the paranoia.

Many of these stereotypes come from old memories and misconceptions, but sometimes they are perpetuated and encouraged by the media, which often reflect the greatest differences between the two solitudes. Nobody in his right mind would deny the fact, for instance, that, during the Québec referendum, most newsrooms in the province were pro-sovereignty. That was even true within the state-run network of Radio-Canada, although the main difference there was that the people who pulled the strings in the newsroom were favourable to the Trudeau government. The disagreement did not necessarily produce unbalanced coverage as much as it generated all-out arguments in newsrooms and accusations of bias on both sides.

Radio-Canada, of course, has always been an exception — perhaps a healthy one that provided some well-needed balance, perspective and, the key, money. If it weren't for the publicly funded network, for instance, several of Brian Mulroney's trips abroad would have gone totally unreported — like the Commonwealth Summit, for instance, which most French news organizations totally ignored as "une affaire d'Anglais."

It is certainly true that "national" Canadian news — as it may be called for lack of a better term — often gets drastically different coverage in Québec than it does in the rest of Canada.

For instance, when Brian Mulroney gave a speech in Hull in which he warned separatists against the possible negative consequences of independence, he made headlines everywhere. But, in French-Canadian newspapers, he was practically accused of invoking the "fear" argument federalists used during the 1980 referendum campaign, while in English-Canadian newspapers, he was generally viewed as having given a powerful, forceful, plausible speech. It is not that the Québécois don't know that separation will be costly. They can see through the glorious rhetoric of the separatist leaders. In fact, fear of the future and losing some of the comforts of life was a major reason for the failure of the 1980 referendum. But Québécois have had enough of being convinced to stay in Canada for all the negative reasons. Those who still favour the federation simply want to know why they should be proud to be Canadian — and even they would like to be left alone to promote their distinctiveness at home.

The differences in perception are apparent in all sorts of other ways. When Jean Chrétien delivered a major speech in Montréal in 1991, before the same crowd and the same journalists, the francophones ended up speaking of his stand on the constitution, while the English media stuck to his economic policies.

And then there are the less subtle ones: the Commonwealth Summit attended by the same prime minister, representing the same country, is given broad coverage in English, whereas "Le Sommet de la Francophonie," just as crucial but with President Mitterrand taking the place of Queen Elizabeth ii, is left off the pages and news bulletins of most English news organizations, while the Québec press pours everything it has into it.

I must admit, however, that more and more, every French Québec media outfit has grown uninterested in things having to do with Canada abroad, even "Le Sommet de la Francophonie." There were no journalists other than the Radio-Canada ones to cover the prime minister's visit to France, for instance, or to cover the seventy-fifth anniversary of the Vimy Ridge victory or the fiftieth of the Dieppe disaster. Why news management decided these were not worthy stories is a little beyond me. And there is unfortunately only one explanation: "Une affaire d'Anglais," as my friend used to say.

It has become too common an excuse for shrugging off assignments and cutting expenses.

But most Québec media follow the ailing Montréal Expos to Los Angeles, San Francisco, and other American destinations eighty-one days of the season. They religiously, of course, tail the "Canadiens de Montréal" and the "Nordiques de Québec." And should a Québec drug pusher be arrested in Miami, they'll be there.

But, somehow, when their Baie Comeau-born prime minister travels, the knee-jerk reaction is to have second thoughts about it. They leave it to Radio-Canada — they can always scalp it for sound — or to Canadian Press. Sometimes — not too often — Canadian Press is represented by a Presse Canadienne reporter, more often by both: evidently the Toronto-run news agency doesn't trust French-Canadian reporters to get the right angle on the news.

Two headline stories in the last year prove the difference between the English- and French-Canadian media. The first, of course, is Mordecai Richler's scathing attack on Québécois in *Oh Canada, Oh Quebec!* The second is the revelation that while still a PQ cabinet minister, Claude Morin met regularly with the RCMP to "exchange information." The difference in the treatment the two men got in the Québec press is living proof of what the Québécois have to fear most about the just and tolerant society they claim to want to create for themselves.

We all know the outrage Mordecai caused in the province with his charges of anti-semitism and phrases depicting French-Canadian society as descendants of prostitutes, "les filles du roi." Richler's words were slightly twisted by the French media on this point. In the same breath he tore into the Loyalists, calling them "adventurers," among other things — his point being that no Canadians had any right to consider themselves superior to others or to immigrants — but the Québec press paid little attention to that detail.

As for the Québécois being anti-semitic, well, Richler did make one huge mistake — or maybe it was a calculated marketing move — when he compared *Le Devoir* of the 1930s to a German Nazi propaganda newspaper. He was exaggerating — for effect, or otherwise — and everyone agrees that Ontario society, for instance, was also anti-semitic in those days — but was he wrong in his basic premise, that Québec was anti-semitic?

I have already had too many arguments — many of them at the Press Club's "French Table" — about this. But what angered me most was that nowhere in the Québec press did anybody give Richler the benefit of the doubt. Nowhere did they say or write what a treasure it was to have such a talented writer not only living in the province, but professing publicly he loved it and French Canadians, in spite of his sharp criticism.

No. They would rather go to their fictitious social barricades and say collectively, and individually: "We are not like that. We do not hate Jews."

And then there was Claude Morin, suave PQ cabinet minister, father of the referendum, the magus with the pipe, the author who wrote a book called *Mes premiers ministres* (*My Prime Ministers*).

A rat, by any other name. He took money from the

RCMP — thousands of dollars he claims he donated to charity — in exchange for information about God knows what.

When the story about Morin became public, the Québec French media were understandably stunned. As I have said to many people since it happened, had I heard the information before, I would have put it away in the same file as reports of UFO sightings.

All to say, it was a helluva story!

I suppose that what threw reporters off was the fact that Morin admitted it. But, as I have found out since, it is true that rumours had been circulating for a while about his involvement with the police, and there remains one unassailable fact: he didn't say a word until he got caught by a Radio-Canada reporter.

And this is where the reaction of the Québec media is interesting, if you compare it with their agitation over Richler's writings.

Day after day, Morin was given an incredible amount of costly newspaper space to clear his name. First, he wrote a piece about how it happened and why he did it. Then he wrote another one, proclaiming that he had given the money to his parish priest.

I'm not referring to his comments to the press, which were themselves given great play in news articles. These were his own explanatory pieces, each of them taking up at least half a page of a full-length newspaper, with little or no editing — as is the rule in the French-Canadian media.

As far as I was concerned, all that came out of the revelations was the fact that Morin had lied several times to the media. That, in itself, is indictable.

To be fair, most editorialists and columnists in the province did not take his side. The fact remains, however that, even if the Québec press did not justify Claude Morin's actions — which would have been a neat trick indeed — it went out of its way to say that what he had done did not diminish his loyalty to his people, his party, or his government.

If that is so, why did René Lévesque go to the washroom, apparently to throw up, as PQ bureaucrat Lorraine Lagacé reported to *La Presse*, when he learned about these exchanges in 1981 — four years after Morin claimed to have informed him of them?

What baffles me today, as I write this, is that by the time you read it, this man may have emerged as some kind of hero or martyr in Québec, like Dollard des Ormeaux, the manufactured hero who was supposed to have given his life to save Montréal from the Iroquois, although historians now consider him to have been a bum the colonists were happy to get rid of.

Everybody was eager to speak of Morin's "loyalty," but hardly anybody took Mordecai Richler seriously when he said he loved French Canadians, wanted to stay in Québec, and thought he was living among some of the most innovative people in the world. In effect, his book was itself an act of loyalty, written in anger but also in love.

The Québec media have a lot of growing up to do. While they have opened themselves to the world, they have shut the doors on English Canada.

True, like all media, they have the right to protect what they perceive to be the interests of their constituents. True, they have a right to expect the same in return from the other side.

In the meantime, though, they are contributing to keeping their people, as Frère Untel put it, in a state of servitude, this time to an ideal of separateness, even if the cost is self-delusion. How else can they justify lambasting a Richler while sparing a Morin?

I feel I'm in mourning, though I'm not sure for what or for whom.

EPILOGUE

ʒʋ   ʒʋ   ʒʋ

There is no doubt about it: the fleur-de-lys is an impressive flag. I get the shivers everytime the French assemble several thousand of them and march down a Montréal street in what seems like an unstoppable tidal wave.

Maybe it's the sky-blue colour, maybe it's the fleurs-de-lys themselves, or maybe it's the white cross that makes the bearers of the flag look like so many crusaders advancing against an unseen and still largely unknown enemy.

Or perhaps Brian Mulroney is right when he says we should not be impressed by parades. Most of us, I suppose, are only human. And most French Canadians are, indeed, moved.

It is only a flag, a piece of cloth, a prop designed by none other than the consummate tyrant himself, Maurice Duplessis. But for many francophones, it is a lifeline; something to hang on to; something they can see, feel, and be proud of.

As you can see, not everything in our past or our current history is — or should be — a source of pride to us.

Far from it. Some truths are hard for all of us to swallow, and public confessions are never as easy to make as the Catholic church made them out to be in private. We can't excuse some of our faults by reciting the rosary and go home feeling cleansed and good about ourselves.

A confession of sorts is, however, a necessary step in our quest for a better understanding of ourselves and, if we're lucky, of others. The introspection of French Canada is a painful attempt at evolution and, yes, even revolution.

One way or another, it will come. This is not a threat, simply a statement of fact. If you are not convinced after reading this book that French Canadians constitute a nation — a people — in their own right, then I have failed.

Divided, but distinct, and with an uncanny ability to band together when times get tough. Throughout our history, past or present, we have often had nothing but the will to survive to keep us going.

Just as Maurice Richard could score goals lying on his back with blood flowing down his face, we French Canadians will keep trying because we feel in our souls that we have no other choice.

We are not a violent people. Quite the contrary. But we are a nation of fighters. We were born and bred to fight, and we will not stop now. When Frère Untel is dead and gone, there will be others to preach the gospel, to shame the people into honouring their duty to their forefathers and their children.

True, we will tell ourselves tall tales, and relive past glories that never were to give our hearts the extra beat, to give our legs the extra step, to give our voices the words that sing. . . . And we will sing on.

If it has to be in Québec only, so be it. If it is so important to the governments and people of Manitoba, Ontario, and New Brunswick that French be eradicated from their communities, so it will be. The last line of defence will be pushed back, but I think it will hold.

In the course of our struggle we, like all nations, have made mistakes, been guilty of gross prejudice, and maintained we were right when we knew we were wrong. But only a desperate people hangs on to lies.

We would rather dream. For many, the dream would magically come true in an independent country. I do not think it is that simple. I do not believe such a drastic move is necessary.

And, to be frank, I don't want to give up on Canada, if only because it's a fine piece of real estate.

I would also be lying if I didn't admit that I feel proud to be Canadian, that over the years I have come to believe that this country, with all its diversity and inherent contradictions, has probably done more to promote human dialogue and understanding than any other on earth.

I don't know any more than you do what the future holds. As I write this, the country is about to embark on yet another round of constitutional talks. I wish I could tell you not to worry, that the Québécois won't separate. I wish I could tell you that, if they choose to do so, everything will go smoothly and nobody will get hurt. But, of course, I can't.

I only know that, like most French Canadians, my heart is torn between a fleur-de-lys and a maple leaf. Maybe my children and yours will cope better with our differences. Maybe, some day, we will decide to live an adventure together.